SOME LETTERS FROM
A SUBALTERN ON THE
WESTERN FRONT

Printed for Private Circulation only

JOHN BALDWIN HOYLE, M.C.
LIEUT., 7th BATT. SOUTH LANCASHIRE REGIMENT

*Born Sept. 16th 1892.   Gazetted Sept. 23rd 1914 ; promoted Lieutenant April 27th 1915
Killed in action near Ovillers-la-Boiselle, July 1st 1916, while acting
as Forward Observing Officer to his Division.*

SOME LETTERS FROM A SUBALTERN ON THE WESTERN FRONT

CHIEFLY TO HIS MOTHER

JULY 1915—JUNE 1916

The Naval & Military Press Ltd

in association with

The Imperial War Museum
Department of Printed Books

Published jointly by
The Naval & Military Press Ltd
Unit 10 Ridgewood Industrial Park,
Uckfield, East Sussex,
TN22 5QE England
Tel: +44 (0) 1825 749494
Fax: +44 (0) 1825 765701
www.naval-military-press.com
www.military-genealogy.com
www.militarymaproom.com

and

The Imperial War Museum, London
Department of Printed Books
www.iwm.org.uk

In reprinting in facsimile from the original, any imperfections are inevitably reproduced and the quality may fall short of modern type and cartographic standards.

Ὅν οἱ θεοὶ φιλοῦσιν ἀποθνήσκει νέος
MENANDER

Yet, O stricken heart, remember, O remember
  How of human days he lived the better part.
April came to bloom and never dim December
  Breathed its killing chills upon the head or heart.

Doomed to know not Winter, only Spring, a being
  Trod the flowery April blithely for a while,
Took his fill of music, joy of thought and seeing,
  Came and stayed and went, nor ever ceased to smile.

Came and stayed and went, and now when all is finished,
  You alone have crossed the melancholy stream,
Yours the pang, but his, O his, the undiminished
  Undecaying gladness, undeparted dream.
R. L. S.

In the time of their visitation they shall shine
WISDOM III, 7

NOTE

*H*ere are collected most of the letters which Jack wrote home during his eleven and a half months service in France. A few have been omitted for various reasons.

He wrote nearly every day, and if there was no letter from him on the breakfast table, there was usually a post card to assure us that all was well.

It will, we think, be plain that the letters are printed not for the public eye, but just for those who loved the writer, for his family first, then for the nearest of his many friends. He had no fear or anxiety for himself, his concern was all for those who sat at home, and his one desire was not to add to the fears he knew were crowding round them. That is why he confined himself almost entirely to the lighter aspects and incidents of warfare, and but rarely touched on the larger and more sombre happenings.

Many of the letters are very slight in texture, while others are little more than a tale retold. But still it seems to us that, taken together, they do form a mirror in which those who knew him may catch reflections of his radiant spirit, of his love for the beautiful which enabled him to find beauty everywhere, of the eagerness and gay courage which never failed him as he followed to the end a road that, until duty pointed, he had never dreamed that he should tread.

E. L. H.
M. K. H.

Scene : A REST CAMP IN FRANCE
Sunday 18*th July* 1915

Dear Mother

It will be somewhere right away from here that I post this as we can only send the field post-card from this place; *that* I hope you will soon receive. It is quite hard to believe we were in familiar Tidworth yesterday afternoon, so vivid are the intervening experiences.

The last preparations were made in feverish haste.... the piano was accepted joyfully by the Church of England Soldier's Institute.... and about five o'clock we paraded, the officers simply loaded down with pack and gadgets. There was a longish wait at the station; the North Lancashires were waiting in one train when we arrived. As each train sailed out the band of some other regiment played "Auld Lang Syne." It was odd to see the usual "to Berlin," etc., chalked on the carriages as one had seen them for months in the illustrated papers; and now one was involved oneself.

At every station where we halted there were crowds of waving and cheering people; it was quite a "huzzah-ride." Hewlett, Ridley, and I were very cheery in our compartment. It was after eleven when we reached the port, where, as I said, so many folks go. I shall never forget the embarcation. We detrained and formed up in absolute silence, and filed along a very long platform which I suddenly recognised from

December 1911 when we sailed for Wengen. Instead of the cattle barge I had expected, there was a trim cross-channel steamer waiting for us, straining at the leash.

There was a clandestine air about the whole business that gave an absurd effect of a rather discreditable undertaking. All lights in the train were extinguished the moment we left the carriages, and the men were hustled across the gangway and herded down below with furtive speed. In the few lights that were shown the faces of the officers looked pale and grim as they moved about the darkened deck. The crowning touch was the arrival of D Company with Winser leading. He is the man of the varied clothing. During the last week or so he has taken to wandering about barracks with a pole like a boy scout's. Last night, armed with his pole and a cap with projecting wings, he suddenly appeared out of the darkness in a circle of lamplight, and turning to guide D Company he looked exactly like a fairy queen in a pantomime.

It was a night of countless stars. As we cleared the harbour we passed a torpedo-boat close by, just a black shape with a trail of foam astern, and judging by the shape of the trail she seemed to be twisting like a snake. The officers went below for some food, and groping down the stairs we trod continually on the men, who perched like flies all about and never seemed to resent our tramplings.

One thought of the light-hearted tourists who had sailed in the same boat. We seemed to be setting out on an unparalleled adventure, unconnected with any serious issues. All the way as we went was the sinister but seemingly lifeless shape of our escort. Eventually we were sailing between long wooden quays while search-lights blinked at us, and the debarcation officer shouted directions through a megaphone.

We trekked off among the usual cobbles and railway lines through the sleeping town. It was about two, and the returning light revealed to our Lancashire labourers the shapes of foreign roofs and shutters. The only sign of life was at a street corner, where a woman straight out of Hogarth held a light to her face and shouted "good-night" and something about Tipperary, with French "r's." We climbed an almost interminable hill of great steepness and reached at last this camp which is on level ground high up. We got the men sorted into their tents, which are not "bells" but those bivouac shelters, and then went through a belt of trees to our own, which are "bells" and brand new, unlike the ones at the Pennings. By this time it was daylight and rather chilly; however we wrapped ourselves in whatever kit we had (the transport with our valises had gone on somewhere) and slept quite well till late in the morning.

We have had a calm and very pleasant day, though it was only comparatively late that leave was given for two officers per Company to go into the town. Personally I have been quite happy up here in such surroundings. We have issued respirators and the "iron" or emergency ration.

On the road that adjoins the camp the bourgeoisie are having their Sunday evening stroll, to the delight of the soldiery. Two of our men I saw keeping up good relations with our allies by saluting a piou-piou.

With our company mess we have made merry sitting on boxes round others up-ended, eating rations supported by reinforcements from the canteen. I did some bacon most successfully this morning on my cooker.

We move, I believe, to-morrow morning, though only Headquarters know where. I don't know when I shall be able to post this.

    No more for the present
      Your loving son
        JACK

BILLETS	7th SOUTH LANCS.
20*th July* 1915	56th INF. BRIGADE
	19th DIVISION
	B. E. F., FRANCE

DEAR MOTHER,

  I am afraid you will have been waiting anxiously for news. The grey shadow of censorship is over us, and Vellacott will be having first go at this.

My last was written in the rest camp at our port of debarcation. On the Monday morning we really set out on our adventures, marching away to a railway station a few miles off; I, of course, with eager eyes gazing at France at last. The men on passing friendly inhabitants would shout "bonn-zoo," to the delight of the latter. It was country not wholly unlike that valley where we drove from Stockbridge to Andover;

but the local touch was given by the tramline on the side of the cobbled road, and then, of course, the buildings are entirely different. There was a long wait at the station, and trains with colossal engines and various troops rumbled past. The men were to travel thirty-six in a truck; it suggested the deportation of the inhabitants of Louvain. It was said that we, too, were going in a truck, but when the train eventually arrived there was a first-class coach. I got sandwiched in with about eight others in a beautiful carriage, nicer than an English one, and we ambled off through a charming country-side that the play of light and cloud made pictures of.

There was some excitement when we found ourselves in sight of the sea again and stopping at a well-known port, as if at the last moment the project was cancelled and they were going to call us back to England after all. I was one of those detailed to superintend the detraining of transport vehicles, one of the things I don't shine at. When the carts were unloaded, the various fatigue parties involved collected under their respective officers (the main body having gone on ahead) and I found myself at the head of an assorted crew with little more than my map to guide them to the village of the billets. The French are doubtless blasé about us now, for there were no shouts of "qu'il est beau" and scattered roses such as Geoffrey had. Picture us setting out through the flat country to an unknown destination. One of the officers asked me if I thought we should put out an advanced guard. It was about five o'clock, and about an hour later the tower and weirdly cowled chimney of a distillery appeared looming out of the trees, and the map showed we were arriving. The groups that composed my posse trekked off towards the billeting areas of their respective companies, and I went out with A Company's contribution to the further end of the village. The men are quartered in the lofts and barns of two farms a hundred yards or so apart, rather different from the friendly cottages of Andover or the stately homes of Clevedon, but they have lots of straw and are quite happy. Hewlett and Ridley are in the family quarters of one farm ; Hughes and I live in a smaller one. We have a capital bedroom each. The vine leaves trail in at my latticed window, and through it you see the red tiles and flapping pigeons, with the farmyard noises and smells coming up from below, just as I have seen it in a hundred French exercise and story books.

There are two old ladies here, dears, both of them, with the kindest hearts. My vocabulary is weak at present, but I can make myself understood. The men are gradually picking up a few scattered phrases. If you would like to make my platoon happy, a consignment of cigarettes—they smoke an abomination called "Woodbine"—would do it. They have to pay through the nose here, and their letters consist largely of quite pitiful appeals.

This letter I find is petering out. There is lots to say, but it must wait. Even if I told you the name of the place it would convey nothing, and I hear fearful tales of the regimental censor.

During the day we alternately route-march and bathe ; the latter where a slow river passes through Constable scenery.

Your letter came to-day, welcome as you can imagine. I love France, as I knew I should. Yesterday morning, during my round of visiting some sentries, I turned into a church and was delighted by the atmosphere of colour and consecrated splendour in so small a village, trumpery and vulgar as much of the decoration was.

Even if I chose I could tell you very little of our movements.

Love to all,

JACK

BILLETS
25th July 1915

DEAR MOTHER

I can only hope that the arrival of three letters at once will cheer you a little for the delay you have had in waiting for one.

What an adventure this is. Very slowly we are approaching the guns, faintly heard on still nights—but sitting at my window that looks out over these pleasant fields, I find it quite hard to realise that this is part of the country the Germans have invaded; that that noise and destruction are really going on these comparatively few miles across the corn that was just now golden in the late afternoon, and that Geoffrey and so many others are there. It gives quite a theatrical effect of being behind the scenes.

We left our first friendly billet a few days ago, with fond farewells between Hughes and self and the two kindly sisters of the little farm. Out we went upon the high road lined with tall trees. It is the oddest thing after months of training, when everything is make-believe, suddenly to see everything done in sober earnest. It was a march of about 14 miles, and the men found it pretty stiff. On these occasions their characters come out pretty clearly, some of them putting up with miles of pain rather than fall out. Will you send some more Homocea? My platoon use it on the march with some success. The part of the day that all of us found a little trying was when we reached our destination and found some hitch in the billeting arrangements, so that we had to go on several more miles. Eventually all was well, and as the light closed in, I conducted my platoon into their farm.

Our billets were very scattered that night—each platoon in successive farms, up a long lane. The officers ate very happily in another, and slept where they could.

We moved on again early next morning for a shorter distance, and arrived here. Most of the Company is in a farm with a fine orchard up the road, but my platoon are here with me and Hewlett. We have managed to secure beds. To-day, after the two days of marching (the men were quite tired) has been a Sabbath rest. Hewlett and I and Ridley, who sleeps next door, go up to the further farm for meals. Several times lately, sitting down in a strange land to café in pretty bowls, I have thought we are an oddly assorted group that circumstances have blown together. And yet one takes this sort of life now as a matter of course. But last night, as Hewlett and I left the top farm to come down here, it did seem a little strange. It was a magical night, absolutely still, with a great moon that turned the corn to silver; the trees stood as if tranced, and then eastward among all that silent beauty, one heard the faint dull percussions, "pup-pup," from along that narrow strip of open ground which the armies have tried in vain during all these months to cross, with an arrested world at gaze.

Needless to say I am vastly happy. Luckily too, my flat feet are absolutely unscathed and carry me on without a blister, It is growing late, or I would go on in greater detail.

To-day I have heard from Arthur, Teddy and Geoffrey.

Best love

JACK

27th July 1915

DEAR MOTHER

I have received your letter asking, as I feared, for news. Also a jolly parcel last night of cocoa complete and chocolate. I shall keep these until we reach the trenches, as we can get more or less anything we want here.

We are sitting round a table under a tree in the orchard, with a pile of the day's letters, censored at last, by us. These are very calm days for us outwardly, for an officer should seldom feel entirely free.

We have breakfast about seven, and other things happen at intervals of an hour, ending in company parade at ten. This, after very minute inspection of arms and kit, peters off into bathing and physical drill. We bathe in a very shallow muddy stream that meanders among the cornfields. The afternoon is usually spent censoring the men's letters. They write copiously, as Donkin said.

Hewlett and I sleep in an estaminet down the road, with a bedroom each. There are farm buildings attached where my platoon sleep on straw. It is absolutely flat country, corn land with scattered farms standing in their orchards and occasional rows of poplarish trees. From the village a quarter of a mile away rise chimneys and hauling machinery. A single line of railway runs through the fields, and any morning you may see a Red Cross train steaming quietly back from railhead. This afternoon I saw a regiment going up to the front all complete, the men dangling their legs from the covered trucks, the transport carts on flat wagons and the officers serene in their passenger coach.

The trains are rumbling past all day long with men and supplies, and their long whistles float on the night air.

There was some excitement yesterday, when an aeroplane appeared in the offing behind us, and the air was filled with puffs of aircraft shells. It was like a firework display very remote. It is reported from official sources that on much of the front there is nothing whatever doing.

We are likely to be here for a day or two now, and they say that the next move is to further billets.

Almost all day we have heard an "intermittent cannonade." The smells of this farm yard are indescribable. We have been driven out of our eating room by the flies. The farm folk too, are not very attractive, which doubtless sounds discouraging, but is of very minor importance. We give the effect of "Where my caravan has rested." The transport are parked in a part of the big orchard that nearly surrounds the farm buildings, and coming in at the gate at meal times, past the little brick shrine of Notre Dame des Affligès, the Company sitting with their mess tins on the grass look like holiday makers.

I have had such nice letters from Uncle James and Auntie Mabel. I am delighted to hear that Billy is a captain, so is old Hewitt of Queen's, whom you may remember as the absentee whose place at the O. R. Dance was taken by Macdonald. He is still with the A.S.C. in Tipperary.

I wonder if my luggage has come home yet. I must not forget the keys. I don't see why I shouldn't have my Sam Browne out here after all.

Enthralling and absorbing as this Great Adventure is, occasionally the idea of home and home-coming comes iuto my mind as something incredibly beautiful.

Best love to all

JACK.

SAME PLACE
29 *Juillet,* 15

Dear Mother

By this time to-morrow we shall be in pastures new. I am at the window of my little room in the Estaminet, and can see the wheat and the rye and some unknown vegetable, past the railway where a troop train has just gone by toward railhead, to the village of rather squalid brick cottages and ugly little church. But beyond, as I saw this afternoon, the country rolls away green and beautiful to a line of hills; beyond that doubtless one would see the war.

Our route march took us this morning through a grimy mining village, very like the ones in Derbyshire round about Swanwick. The afternoon was spent as usual round our table in the orchard snoozing and inspecting the men's letters. These are very dull on the whole, consisting mainly of applications for money and "cigs.," and complaints of the difficulties of intercourse with the natives; some though are well written and quite a number are intimations of regret and hope and affection, that, coming from these outwardly rough people, are very moving.

Punch was very welcome. Also the cake that arrived to-day, and delighted the officers. Hewlett has the funniest servant from across the Atlantic, old enough to be our father, who when asked to do something says, "why certainly;" before the war he was the chauffeur of a licentious millionaire and earned mints of money for practically no work; he must be a first-class man or he would not now be the extremely conscientious and hard-working servant he is on ten shillings a month.

As far as we know, we are not going far to-morrow. Isn't this the strangest journey, slowly approaching the guns whose muffled explosions we hear from our orchard? I am feeling very "hearty" about it.

Will you thank father very much for his letter. I should like some more Homocea and some plaister for my men's feet.

There goes another troop train.

JACK

BILLETS
30th July 1915

DEAR MOTHER

We are comfortably installed in our new billet, but I believe we move on about three miles to-morrow.

We got here about midday; it has been a hot morning and the men seemed very tired. But it was an attractive farm we got them into, and the Company Cooker was wheeled into the orchard soon enough. We ourselves are sleeping in houses at the edge of the town, and in one of them we got some lunch; the occupier is a schoolmaster, driven from some town nearer the frontier, I forget the name, at the beginning of the war. He walked for miles in one of those crowds of refugees.

Seeing the letters and inspecting the men's feet were the duties of the afternoon. After tea, which our servants made in the little yard under the vines, Ridley and I went into the town to buy supplies. There are hosts of Indian troops here and several hospitals. I loved the town of course, tho' like others I've seen it looked slovenly. The most amusing moment was when Ridley went into a butcher's for some bacon. It was a brightly painted shop, white, with ribbons and other decorations, including a veiled chandelier; the back scene and wings were in keeping with the general effect; the front was entirely open to the street. At Ridley's entrance Madame, rather in the grand manner, sailed up beaming; on the left were the two daughters, about twenty-five, sitting together on chairs arranged slantwise to the street, sewing at apparently the same piece of work and much delighted at the beautiful officer; it was more stagey and absurd than anything I've seen in shops. We came back simply loaded with parcels. On the whole I like the women in the shops; they are almost always bright and gracious.

We are now waiting for supper. Ridley and I are going to sleep at the schoolmaster's, but we feed at this little farm next door to the men. It is absolutely flat country, cornfields as usual, and quaint farms all about; occasionally a big canal with a row of fine trees. The guns were remarkably plain when we arrived, tho' we had only gone nine miles. They reminded me of blank artillery ammunition I've heard on field-days.

They say we aren't moving to-morrow after all, which is good news, as we like this place. We weren't sorry this morning at breakfast to be leaving that farm where was "infinite torment of flies" and sharp-tempered women and crying children lived in slovenliness unspeakable.

The night has now passed, but I will tell later of anything that happens to-day.

JACK

BILLETS
1st August 1915

DEAR MOTHER

We all like this place immensely.

Coming from the house where Ridley and I sleep down to our eating room in this farm yesterday morning, for a calm unhurried breakfast, with sunshine all round, was more like the beginning of a holiday or a reading party than anything else. We had a kit inspection and a very jolly bathing parade in one of the several rivers in these parts; it was rather like a canal, so that one could dive straight in, the only disadvantage being the mud you encountered getting out. The chief duties at present are feet and kit inspection and bathing. This morning I came down early and scrambled eggs for the officers' breakfast. We were inspected this morning by General —— who commands the Corps of Indians to which we are at present attached. We stood in line in the road while he and staff passed slowly down, his car creeping behind; then the officers went along to the end and stood round, while it became more and more apparent that he was going to shake hands and ask some well-chosen question of each of us. All he wanted to know was how long we had served. Also he recommended frequent route marches during the periods of billets.

Sitting here in the orchard we are vividly reminded of the European situation by very considerable artillery "liveliness," a series of terrific explosions. Last night, going back to our beds, we stood in the road and watched the flashes light the sky.

I must now go up to Headquarters with the letters.

JACK

BILLETS
2nd *August* 1915

DEAR MOTHER

I have just had your letter, for which very many thanks, and also the Cooker refill, Homocea, etc., besides *Punch*. I give my folk Homocea in the halts when we trek between billets. On the whole I think you might discontinue sending *Punch*. Both Hughes and Hewlett get it. After I had written, the latter issued an edict against largess of Woodbines by platoon officers, but these, which I gratefully acknowledge, will get to the men somehow.

There was the usual physical drill and bathing and foot inspection this morning; in the afternoon all subalterns paraded under the Machine Gun Officers for instruction in the working of that weapon, while the companies route marched under the higher commanders. "A" Company took an axe with them, as the way went through a forest; one of our chief difficulties is firewood; the inhabitants need their scanty stock, but a good deal of filching goes on, and any time during meals enraged or appealing peasants may turn up with tales of woe. As a result of the instruction I now feel competent to fire, and if necessary disable, a M.G. There was a little thunder and a violent shower this afternoon, otherwise it is very sunny and dry.

We are due to move to-morrow from this pleasant place to billets about three miles off. Ridley and I have lodged very comfortably with the schoolmaster and his sister, who are the kindest people.

The Indian troops are very picturesque. They have some cavalry bivouacked in a field near our farm. One sees them carrying beautiful brass jars. They have rigged up swinging beams over the wells, devices that remind me of photographs from Egypt, imported local colour well acclimatized, as if it had been there from time immemorial. It was odd this morning to hear an Indian sergeant giving commands in English; usually we hear oriental chatterings. I long to ask them if they like mangoes, my one Hindustani sentence.

Hughes reported at breakfast time that he had seen a Zeppelin chased by an aeroplane, but he always has lots of sensational reports.

I long to tell you exactly where we are, but shades of the prison house close round even my unmilitary pen. In future I think I shall perpetrate puns, the crucial words bounded by dots.

                       Love to all

                              JACK

Don't put in Brigade or Division.

3rd August 1915

DEAR MOTHER

We had expected to be gone by now, but are still here, and may remain so. I think we are waiting for the evacuation of our intended billets.

The war, on the western front at any rate, seems to have been at a standstill the last day or two; we haven't heard a sound; only at night walking back to our beds at the outskirts of the town we see the sky to north and east flashing and quivering. The weather has broken somewhat.

This morning we subalterns carried on with the machine guns; Perry and I receiving instruction from a sergeant who last autumn was a private in my platoon, aided by a lance-corporal who was also in my platoon at Andover, and who since then was reduced to the ranks for general idleness aud inefficiency, regaining his stripe the other day at Tidworth. Our new Transport Officer, a middle-aged gentleman with a son in the trenches, lunched with us, and in the afternoon Hewlett gave us and the N.C.O.'s a disquisition from a pamphlet on trench life and how to conduct it.

On this evening of wind and showers and premature twilight, one's mind naturally travels back to this time a year ago, when we all, with bated breath, were waiting for the issue. I had gone over to the Wadsworths', rather a furtive flight from overtaking unpleasantnesses, as I half knew it to be; but there was no escape, and I was soon back in a strangely altered world on which the blow had fallen. I remember my surprise at the general bad temper into which my amiable and placid Europe was breaking; and now it seems so obvious and inevitable that we were blind not to have anticipated all.

Would you, instead of *Punch*, send the *Bystander* and any of the following:—*Sporting and Dramatic, Illustrated London News, New Statesman* (for my particular benefit).

JACK

4th August, 1915

DEAR MOTHER

I am so glad that my letters are finding their way home. Many thanks for your long one just received. It is thrilling to hear about Bakewell.

We are likely to be here for some time yet before we reach the trenches at all. After that this may be our permanent home between whiles. As we of " A " Company are very comfortable here we don't quarrel with the arrangement. I had occasion to go this morning to the Brigade Office to draw money for the men's pay from the field cashier—a bank clerk in uniform. The office is in part of a graciously designed house standing back from the road among tall and elegant trees, surrounded by a moat that a bridge of delicate ironwork spans; the whole most harmonious and fair to see.

We paid the men out in the afternoon from a table carried into the orchard ; this is always a joyous event for them in these days when there is no longer the regular Friday paying. Later I had to see the Adjutant in an interview that involved the discovery of an omission of mine in the past, and which I rather dreaded;

however, Vellacott wasn't at all put out, and being alone we had a discussion about the war and its probable developments. During the afternoon our long expected hampers from Fortnum and Mason arrived, containing food of all sorts, on which we intend to run our mess. Drunk with sight of power we nearly invited some officer to dinner on the spot. In the end, however, I scrambled some eggs which we had in hand; this stunt of mine is always applauded.

This morning—one night having elapsed—we had the usual physical drill and bathing in the restored sunshine. At the moment Hewlett is taking the Company outside our windows in handling of arms, in his best parade ground Hun-like manner, which his six months on the square under Old Army N.C.O.'s taught him—a now almost forgotten art. Ridley and Hewlett and I are getting on extremely well together, one could hardly ask for better company; we wish that we were in a mess by ourselves. Life is very calm at present, we might be at Tidworth, and I haven't heard a gun for days.

I get opportunities of learning French conversation just now with the schoolmaster whose house Ridley and I sleep in. My vocabulary is absurdly small, but we struggle along somehow. He impresses our servants immensely by knowing a little English, also he gives them coffee in the morning when they come to wake us. Sometimes I find him reviving old days, sitting at his table with two expressionless-voiced children learning to read.

Your loving son
JACK

BILLETS

7th August 1915

Dear Mother

Many thanks for yours of a day or two ago. As you see, we have rest for our feet now-a-days. It was a case of nightly pitching our wandering tent some time back. We didn't proceed towards the trenches in a straight line from our railhead, but changed direction altogether on the second day.

Yesterday morning we did field operations against our machine gunners. They had got into part of a forest, and A Company had to cut off their retreat while the other three Companies dredged the wood for them like a line of beaters. Eventually it was rather a fiasco, as we misunderstood orders and started off half-an-hour late; otherwise we should have caught them nicely jumbled together in a road. There was a terrific shower in the middle, just as I was trying to write a message. Faintly in the distance we heard the guns again, after several days' silence; our make-believe warfare seemed odd to such an accompaniment.

Winser dined with us, and Perry, who has revealed a genius for cookery, rose to the occasion. When you hear that we had soup, omelette (by Madame), mince with bits of toast, roast potatoes and cauliflower, trifle, sardines on toast, and fruit, you won't feel anxious about us on the score of starvation. True, it was a bit extra special, but that is just as well.

We feel we are getting in touch with things now, as two regiments of the Brigade have been in the trenches and we have reports of their doings. Indeed the happy day is named for us.

We have made a capital field kitchen in the men's orchard so that they can have some variety in their dinners, as the field cookers only make stews. This morning we had bathing as usual. It is a slow deepish river and gives very pleasant bathing; only getting out the mud is disgusting and covers you unless you wriggle ashore over the reeds like a prehistoric beast landing. The troops enjoy it immensely.

Yesterday the cake arrived; there has been no opportunity of eating it yet, but it looks excellent; very many thanks. Later I shall probably send for some books, but I am getting practically no reading done; I have "The Egoist" out here, bought before I left England for use in the campaign, besides some Shelley and, you will regret to hear, Shaw.

The Rowntree Queen Chocolate is first rate; the cocoa I am keeping for the trenches. Will you thank Margaret for her long and delightful letter, which I read with the greatest pleasure.

JACK

BILLETS
8th August 1915

DEAR MOTHER

I received yesterday innumerable parcels from home, mostly from Father; they were extremely welcome. Eva Birley very kindly sent food, and Mildred a letter. There came also *Punch* from you; we hadn't seen the latest *Punch* yet, but I suppose from now on you won't send it, according to my request of a few days back.

I was orderly officer yesterday and had to turn out the squad "at frequent and irregular intervals." About half-past nine it was a night that followed a stormy sunset with a sky of wonderful stars ; but the wind was up and thin clouds scudding across, and by half-past eleven, as I left the edge of the town to go up to H.Q., it was pitch dark, and the Indian sentry's orientalised "halt, who goes there," as I passed General——'s headquarters, sounded weirdly out of the blackness. It struck me afterwards that I should never have thought a year ago that I should be walking at dead of night in France, in the uniform of an officer, and challenged by the voice of an unseen Indian, who gave the familiar formula a chanting note as of an old refrain. The night would have been darker still were it not for the illuminating bombs, all along the eastern horizon and northwards, that continually set parts of the sky flickering. By sleeping in uniform I managed to wake up again at half-past three and stole out a second time to see if I could catch the squad napping. They turned out however very promptly. After that I undressed and slept soundly till I went up to this farm to scramble the eggs for breakfast.

Hewlett and I are now in the orchard, Hewlett in a wonderful trench coat lined with sheep-skin and a leather aeroplane skull helmet ; beyond the hedge are the cornfields, golden in a strong light, with a dark wood behind of tall trees all blown one way; not far off rises the parish church, with a large and ornate tower, the most distinctively foreign thing in the landscape perhaps ; it is an ugly modern building, and I was rather put to the other night by our schoolmaster, who extolled it as the worthy handiwork of the supreme contemporary architect, one Cordonnier.

I went into the town this morning—it is a marveelious place,[1] as the man said—intending to search out Billy's billet, as I knew his Brigade had recently arrived. As it happened I met him walking with a brother officer, buying mess supplies.

As captains are three a penny in these days his military decorations didn't look exceptional. He seemed quite happy and very fit. They left England a few days after us, and followed on to this town by a slightly different route.

I must stop to catch the post.

JACK

11th August 1915

DEAR MOTHER

At midnight we slip away from this place to billets nearer up. The advanced party, consisting of Lumley and a few cyclists who went ahead to arrange accommodation, say there is nothing noticeable there besides a ruined chapel[2] of very ancient date. We shall arrive at dawn and proceed to bivouac ; we made one this morning with rifles and oil-sheets.

Yesterday we had operations in the forest, chasing B Company, who represented the vanguard of a large force, into the bend of a river. The forest is pierced with shooting rides which of course make beautiful straight vistas in some places. Through the summer woods we went with the shade and splashes of sunlight

[1] manifestly Merville, and [2] Vieille Chapeell

playing about us, and enough crackling of twigs to betray any advance. As it happened, A Company met with no opposition, as B retired on to their second line before we came up with them. The fog of war comes on one pretty thick in a big wood, and indeed it muddled a sergeant of ours so completely that I found him, early on in the advance, manoeuvring his platoon with loud shouts till he got it at right angles to the true direction and straying out along a ride, simply asking to be caught by the machine guns which the enemy were known to have. At the pow-wow in the evening, when we sat in a field at H. Q. by a lily pond, the Company was praised for its admirably conducted advance. All the time they were talking the sun, setting half obscured, sent magnificent colours across the cornfields, and a bank of soft clouds in the east was flushed with pink and changed exquisitely every moment. Myriads of stars came out afterwards and seemed to hang without a flicker, and as Ridley and I had our nightly walk to our billet the world seemed asleep, except for the flashes of the illumination bombs, eastward in front, and northwards where Geoffrey is.*

I shall be sorry to leave this place, where we have been very happy, but it is quite on the cards that we shall have this farm as our permanent station. We shall have a calm day to-morrow, and I shall write about a midnight flit.

JACK

---

* He did not know then that his younger brother lay dead at Hooge in Flanders. Geoffrey had fallen in action two days before.

FRESH BILLETS
August 12th 1915

Dear Mother

This is as odd a position as ever I was in, and yet I don't feel as if anything unusual was afoot.

We rested yesterday afternoon and Ridley and I took an affectionate leave of our schoolmaster. We had supper in leisure and peace in our billet, and after strolling about under the stars in the orchard we fell in—at eleven o'clock. The regiment eventually gathered itself together, and we slithered along the treacherous pavé of the sleeping town and out to the the flat unhedged roads beyond.

It was a very still night, with of course, the usual star-shells, which seemed incredibly near. After what seemed more than the advertised six miles, we reached in the faintly growing light the village mentioned in my last. Lumley, who had done the billeting, was here seen flitting about in a state of great importance. He mistook me for an N.C.O.—as I was carrying one of the men's rifles—and told me off violently for being in his way. We had overshot the mark a bit, and after a halt we about turned and made off down the road that led to our billets. The buildings loomed strangely in the half light; on the left was a large church, roofless, with a startling display of daylight through its clerestory windows. On the right was a granary or something similar, with what seemed jagged rents in the walls, and the shutters hanging half unhinged. We reached at last, about half-past three, a farm where two of our platoons went in.

Hughes' and mine were led on to one at the other side of the road. I was aware of a barn end on to the road, with a rough ladder leading from the ground, through a battered opening, to a loft. The men were offered the choice of that shelter or the orchard, and voted instantly for the latter. The hurried glance at the orchard I took before bringing them in confirmed my impression of the desolation I was nearing. Not a blade of grass was left in the hardened soil, and there were many signs of previous occupation. However the men were glad to get down anywhere. Hughes and I then went back to the other farm, which is our head-quarters, We entered a little square farm-yard, with outbuildings of protruding eaves all round, surrounding a very offensive wilderness of manure and garbage. On the cobbles was a stove with a make-shift chimney, very high and rickety, that lost itself in a network of scraggly wires that hung across part of the yard. Coming out again, we passed the farmer and his wife, old, silent, and grim—sinister figures in the dawn; the smells of the place were indescribable, and there was the same soil bereft of grass and evidence of many birds of passage. Then, *faute de mieux*, we officers crossed the road and lay down in a patch of soil among the corn; there seemed to be a faint attempt at turnip-growing, but we took no notice of that. The transport with our valises was nowhere to be seen, but I had all I wanted in my pack. The sun was just warming the world as we dozed off, and the pale colours that began to light the trees and fields showed the countryside far prettier than we had imagined. Happening to wake about five, I took a stroll over to my platoon. The village did indeed look oddly broken down; but though it was shells that accounted for the church further back, general decay seemed the cause here. The men looked so quaint huddled in every attitude under their greatcoats, with their rifles and equipment grouped about the disconsolate trees of that grass-less orchard. I had another snooze, and then Hewlett and I wandered round trying to arrange where everything should be. The place was so dirty that it was only from sheer necessity that anything ought to be there at all. Later we roused the men and afterwards breakfasted quite comfortably in the farm parlour. The old woman is a vixen, and the old man doubtless a spy. I had an absurd argument with them about a place for the officer's kitchen; the girl was more amenable and we won. You never knew such smells, or such a slovenly place.

We have been hanging on here all morning expecting to be sent up to learn the way to the trenches, but no orders were forthcoming till the afternoon. We go up to-night; Hewlett is going ahead to meet us there; Perry has gone to learn the way and conduct us to a rendezvous. Ridley will parade the company this evening and we shall make the last stage of this memorable journey. I feel as if it was a field-day, only more interesting and far greater fun.

I enjoyed your last letter so much. The Sam Browne would really be useful. And I should particularly like my canvas bucket

Now for the Hun. In the best of spirits.

JACK

HERE A FEW
LETTERS ARE
OMITTED

17th August 1915

DEAR MARGARET

I feel for you so much just now. In a letter written last week Mother said she feared you wouldn't have very cheerful birthdays this year; that was before we knew.

For you who have to sit at home these things must be almost intolerable. We who are out here are spared much of the pain. I cannot realise that Geoffrey is numbered among them whose warfare is accomplished, like those others, English and German, who lie in the thousand hasty graves we saw all around the trenches where we were last week. It was so strange then to watch the war being carried on, while just beyond the front parapet were a row of the little graves, all with their wooden crosses and flowers and simple decorations, of those who had gone before. If I saw some of you I should realise it more.

But aren't you proud also? Could a life have been given more willingly or in cheerfuller faith? I know that this thought will help to heal the wound.

To-day is your birthday, dear Margaret. Lift up your heart. "Out of our agonies comes victory."

Your loving brother

JACK

BILLETS
21st August 1915

Dear Mother

I am so sorry I didn't get a letter off this afternoon. And this must only be a short note, as I am off to bed.

It seems the most natural thing in the world to be back here again, in what seems a zone far from the noise of the archers. To-morrow I am getting what I wanted. The officers are going up in relays to the trenches to spy out the land unhampered by their platoons and companies. Ridley, Hughes and I go to-morrow for a day or two, setting out in a motor bus. So don't worry if there is a gap in the arrival of my letters. It may be difficult to write from there.

We have just read about the " Arabic." We saw her sailing out from Liverpool seven years ago on our first family trip to Ireland.

Your letter made me so happy when you said that you felt no bitterness ; and how glad you must be to have heard so much about the glorious end. I only wish you wouldn't feel anxious about me. I have no anxiety about myself.

Good-night. Love to all,

Jack

BILLETS
24th August
Tuesday

Dear Mother

I got back this morning from the trenches where we were with Indians, not Arthur's, but hill-men from the north. I was hoping to hear about Geoffrey and my hopes were more than fulfilled.

For I found your letter of the 20th, in which you told of how you had visited Sherwood Forester Officers. I am so proud of my brother and feel very small and humble beside him. What a comfort it must have been to hear so much and such pleasant information. I can just see Geoffrey shouting at the Germans in their own tongue. He was always in the know about aeroplanes; our study at Rugby was littered with aviation periodicals. Isn't it fine to think that they were so well satisfied with his work!

I suppose Geoffrey's development came late, and when it did come, see how it has blossomed. Happy would anyone be to have achieved so much.

I have had sweet letters from Auntie Katie and from Mildred and Eva.

After to-day I will carry on with my letters as usual. I have told you nothing of our doings lately, but I know that you will be ready to hear them. To-day my thoughts are full of Geoffrey.

Your loving

Jack

BILLETS

26th August 1915

Dear Mother

I had hoped to write a long letter to-day, but as it happens I am Orderly Officer, and this afternoon have to take out forty ruffians who tried to evade a route march this morning, half-broken-down supporters of a sick parade. Happily, I shall have a horse.

You will have gathered that the day after we arrived in rather dilapidated billets in the village of ancient date, the Company moved up for a day or two in the trenches, the last stage of the journey. That seems so long ago that I almost forget what happened. But I remember that as we marched through the gathering darkness, we seemed to come quite suddenly from a land of happy farms and corn-fields to a growing desolation of empty walls and broken roofs, very dark and forlorn. At one corner a tall spreading cross reared its image intact out of chaos. Star shells were flickering continually. We found our guide at last, and filed down the long, long, communication trench. It was a strange journey. Rifles cracked nearer and nearer, and the war seemed to be everywhere and all about us. It seemed a long time before we were installed behind the bank of sandbags that helps to keep England from Germany.

As the flares went up you saw the surprised up-turned faces of us new-comers in a weird lime-light setting of light and shade, yellow sandbags, and their grotesque shadows. We were there two days with these cheery Irishmen. The subalterns of the Company we were attached to were very friendly and volunteered information of every kind.

There was complete calm on both sides, and watching the peaceful unconcerned life that went on behind the shelter of the parapet, you would never have thought the chief European powers were locked in vital struggle. Only the surrounding devastation was impressive.

Just behind us were the ruins of a village, and you saw the remains of a chapel that had only been finished a short time back, a hapless new building that after about a year's life was completely destroyed in the middle of March, the officers told us.

There had also been a large house (in the dark as we came through it might have been the ruins of a Roman villa) and it went to my heart to discover next morning the trace of a little box border along what had been a path, such as you and Margaret might have walked on in thin slippers. Can you imagine a trench through the bottom of the drive at home, regardless of the gateposts, and all the garden trampled in mud and planks, while stray bullets cracked across the lawn at men going to fill their water bottles from the tap under the terrace?

We shared duties with the Irish officers, and at one time on the second night I was in charge of the Company front, armed with the pistol that fires star shells. We also crept out to a listening post (very near our parapet) and a few yards beyond; it feels so strange to be on that no-man's land, just as one used to feel walking along railway lines.

I have a vivid impression of my first look across the parapet the night we arrived. One was aware of long grass that disappeared in mist, and vague shapes of trees ; beyond that a complete blank.

On the Saturday night we returned to our village and had a very quiet time. Most of us slept out in a corn-field, very happily. It was on the afternoon after our return that father's telegram came.

One of our guns was moved quite near us one day and the air was split. On another day the Huns apparently got the range of another gun, and we were aware, while bathing, of events in the neighbourhood. Indians were seen running from a farm in all directions (one came back for his dinner to the general delight) ; there was some smoke and I saw an enormous divot of something. In another moment the firing stopped.

On the Friday night we marched back to our old billets outside this town. Have you guessed the name yet ? On Sunday, Ridley, Hughes and I, with representatives of the other Companies and other Regiments, set off on a bus to be attached to another Regiment for a day or two (little Indians). At Brigade H.Q. we left the bus and had to walk some two miles. We went through a small town where what had been a large church stood in a square, wrecked. It was astonishing to see shops carrying on when their top stories and the houses on either side were in ruins. There are countless instances of this spirit that adversity cannot break. We saw children playing outside their farm only half a mile from the H.Q. of the Battalion in the trenches.

Some of us got in a panic lest we hadn't brought enough food ; we had to ration ourselves, and all we could carry things in was our packs. Accordingly I arrived before their Colonel with an enormous loaf wrapped up in newspaper, bought hurriedly on the way. The Colonel was a most charming and distinguished looking old gentleman. He leaned gracefully against a large dug-out that some of his men were working at, and suggested the *ancien regime*, sublime above the artisans. Actually I believe he isn't so nice as he looks. Ridley and I were detailed off together under the wing of a Company officer. It was a very enjoyable two days, and we learnt a lot surrounded by those dark smiling faces. I was so often reminded of Arthur, hearing the officer talk Hindustani. On the second afternoon word came up along the telephone of the sinking of all those German ships in the Gulf of Riga. Somewhere along the line we had heard cheering in the afternoon like the noise of a distant football match; the news explained it. After dark we raised a rather feeble demonstration ourselves, and abuse in English slang was hurled back. We had rather a fiasco with a rocket. The Divisional General had ordered two to be sent up for some reason from our Company. The officer had never tried them before; the first, after disreputable wobbles, gave it up and dropped from no height at all a few yards behind our own trench, where it burned brilliantly for some minutes with a column of lighted smoke. I expected a violent fusillade from the enemy M.G.'s, but nothing happened.

One took glances through one's periscope at their lines. Across a waste stretch of long grass with an occasional ditch and straggled hedge (a tract that looked as if no attention had been paid to it for centuries, rather nondescript and by suggestion sinister) you saw their bank of sandbags, just like ours. It seemed as if nothing ever stirred behind them, and doubtless ours give the same effect. At times there is absolute peace and quiet in the trenches; there is an occasional surprise bullet, often not even that; you don't notice them after a while. Also at times a lonely shell passes overhead, crackling and tearing its way to some unseen target behind. The surrounding country is utterly forlorn; it isn't so much the trampled ground as the blighted trees, which are melancholy to a degree.

We got back here on Tuesday morning after a lovely bus-drive. We seemed to be back in complete civilisation, among our soup squares and enamel mugs. Hewlett and Perry with others went off the same morning for their turn in the trenches.

Since then we have all been learning about bombs and their manipulation.

I have had letters from you and Father and Aunt Mamie. Old Esson is a brick; I will certainly write. How beautiful about the old ladies and their ancestor. I have also heard from Teddy. I had occasion to interview Vellacott this morning, and as I left Headquarters he got out of the orderly-room window and came after me to ask if it was my brother. Having met you that day he asked that I should send you his sympathy.

Ridley's brother is wounded in the Dardanelles. I am wondering about Varvill, whose Regiment has had a number of casualties out there.

We are shortly going a route march into the forest, taking our tea out.

Your loving son

JACK

28th *August* 1915

DEAR MOTHER

Many thanks for your various letters. The latest contains that thrilling extract from his servant's letter. I have just heard from Jack King, who writes from Windermere to express his sympathy with us all. Kind Mrs. Smith of Andover also writes and says, "I think so much of your Mother and I would like to send her a message of sympathy." I have heard too from little Burroughs, the Dean of Hertford, Oxford, whom I met at Swanwick.

We are having true August weather; it is shocking to think that in just such conditions they made the Retreat last year. Bathing just now is a joy. Yesterday afternoon we did a route march with transport complete; dusk was beginning when we reached a cross-roads in the forest and cooked a late tea. You should see these straight roads that cut such beautiful vistas through the delicate trees; it is a picture on a mellow August afternoon. It was dark as we came home, with a great moon burnishing the corn sheaves; the men sang the bibulous songs they sang months ago, and which were one of my first impressions of them at the Pennings.

This afternoon Hewlett on his horse and Ridley and I on bicycles took tea in the forest. In among the tree stems was absolute silence and the Greek mind would have pictured dryads in the deepening shade; outside was the hum of an aeroplane and a popping of anti-aircraft guns.

We are due for the trenches early next week, but I believe we start taking over by being in the Divisional Reserve, which means more billets. Undoubtedly there is a fascination about the trenches.

I have just received the Bystander and a very excellent looking Dingley Cake.

Some rain is falling, badly needed.

Your loving son

JACK

3rd September, 1915

DEAR MOTHER

We set out yesterday afternoon an untried and irresponsible party, as it now seems; and to-day's rainy dawn found us trudging back on the muddy roads, war-battered veterans.

With B Company we went up as a working party to the Divisional trenches. On the way it began to rain and we prepared our minds for a night of it. The evening set in as we wound over a rough stony road through country that war had changed so oddly, filling orchards with transport, sticking up military sign-hands, and scarring gardens and cornfields with redoubts and trenches and entanglements. Somehow the occasion was more convincing and realistic than previous ones, and when, after an R.E. officer had picked us up at the rendezvous, we proceeded in the gathering dark by platoons, dimly seen, one felt quite impressed. By now we were in the land of tumbled walls, and roofs a network of beams against the sky. Hewlett and I both thought the country more desolate than any we had seen. The platoons nearly lost each other at one point and I found myself trying to keep three-quarters of the Company connected. We reached the spot where tools were dealt out to us and proceeded, dodging round shattered cottages, into the communication trench. We have only done this business twice before, but it seemed as if we had often and often begun winding among sand-bags through orchards. Once again was the effect of the war everywhere. We reached the line of trench in question, while the R.E. officer gave the platoons their jobs. I got my orders eventually and we emerged from the trench to the ground behind. Our job was to fill sand-bags for the R.E. (who chattered and talked in loud voices all the time) and to pile up earth for them by the trench they were working on. I remember being half-consciously amused at the way my folk craned their necks forward, bursting with eagerness to know what was expected of them. They got going with the sand-bags rather well when once they realised they weren't actually digging a trench. Round us were the usual sights and sounds of these nights, occasional shots from snipers or excited sentries, isolated explosions that I put down to trench mortars, and the star shells, when we would all stand motionless like the tranced court of the Sleeping Beauty. A search-light began performing later, and then followed our baptism of fire. A German machine gun, either practising on some target behind or else searching a piece of ground for possible prey, opened fire in our direction. Lying flat we were quite safe because of the breastwork a few yards in front. But bullets often sound nearer than they are, and to our unaccustomed ears it was us they were looking for with peculiar vindictiveness.

But here is Perry, taking the letters up to H.Q. I will continue later.

JACK

BILLETS
8th September 1915

DEAR MOTHER

I have been very bad at letters lately. On Saturday I merely dropped a post card because Hewlett wanted me to go with him to the neighbouring town,* and I thought I might as well get away for an hour or two.

It is too bad ; the censorship is becoming much stricter apparently and I shall have to leave out a lot ; the only consolation is that you will know it is my necessity, not choice.

* Bethune.—The place, like the others, was identified from later information

I left off in the middle of my last letter just as the machine gun was beginning, and I said we were quite safe had we known it, and there is nothing to prove they were after us ; had they known we were there they would have gone on ; instead of which, after a few minutes we heard the shots sweeping away to the flank, and then they stopped, whereupon we resumed work. The experience was worth it.

The other incident of the evening is temporarily censored. It was late when we collected our tools and stole away. Leaving the firing line gives one an absurdly safe feeling, as if no projectile devised by man could reach you. Hewlett, who had occasion to stop behind a bit, lost the turning on the road and we had to go on without him. I thought he might be wandering anywhere in the rain, but there was nothing to be done. I can see us now, winding slowly back along the muddy road in the rain-swept dreary dawn. It was full daylight when we got in, and shortly after we had dismissed I was relieved to hear the hoofs of Hewlett's horse.

On Thursday night we went out again to a different spot, to carry on with the digging of a trench which another regiment of the Brigade had started. We had to plough through a road at one point ; it is curious to see geography pushed aside so violently. Our men worked well, we all thought. Snipers' bullets cracked and whistled and a few shells came overhead, from the unknown to the unknown.

Here again I must stop for the post. I managed a meeting with Vaudrey yesterday.

JACK

9th September 1915

DEAR MOTHER

I have received various things from home including to-day the Bystander and New Witness; there was a cake, and from father ear-protectors and refills of various kinds. Do you know who was the sender of a parcel from Bakewell containing sweets and general delicacies? I couldn't recognise the writing, but it was extremely welcome and is being reserved for the trenches.

I read in yesterday's Times a few paragraphs about Gilbert Talbot, who died very heroically. I recollect him one morning at Cambridge. The Oxford speaker came over to our Union, and I was asked to breakfast in the elder Grose-Hodge's rooms next day.

I have just had a letter from Mrs. Kentish-Wright, Varvill's aunt; she says she sympathises specially with you as she lost a son earlier in the war.

Meanwhile the golden September days are drowsy enough when one is not actively engaged. Walking out into our orchard, even though we were up at the trenches a few hours before, I have once or twice wondered if it is really possible that so fair and calm a world contains such doings those few miles off. The guns, which are of course quite near, disturb us very little; several times daily you recognise the sound of anti-aircraft machine guns, the rapid discharge followed by the more leisurely explosions, and round the aeroplane you see pretty white puffs by day, and against the rose-flushed evening clouds delicate curls of dark grey. But that is all. In this farm, that stands in a lane, we are aloof from the rush of life ; a few yards away the traffic of the war whirls past, motor ambulances, lumbering supply lorries, and gilded staff officers in their cars.

The sky is settled and I think we are in for a spell. Hughes and I went up this morning with a platoon for more bomb throwing. Little Williams commands the Brigade bombers now, and we found him this morning finishing breakfast among his officers in quite a handsome farm. They seem quite a happy community. Can I have Masefield's "Captain Margaret" and "Multitude in Solitude"? They may be got in Nelson's 7d. edition. Will you thank father immensely for the cigarettes and tobacco.

No more for the present
JACK

11th September 1915

DEAR MOTHER

We got back this morning from another working party expedition. We are getting quite used to these dissipated returns through the morning mists, leaving the cracks and flickers and the stealthy labours of the firing line, where the poplars are vague shapes against their starry background, for the quiet village and this billet with its mellowing fruit trees, very still in the early morning sunshine; and the happenings you have just left still within earshot, quite honestly like a fantastic dream.

Last evening indeed I thought would be rather trying. Hewlett had gone on in the afternoon, and

I brought the Company up. We reached the rendezvous where a deserted pub with a door perforce ever open stands at a corner, but there was no Hewlett and no R.E. guide. I knew I was at the place stated in Orders but it was conceivable that this was only a rough indication. Various devices were adopted, I stood at the corner, connected with the Company which was further down the road by a string of orderlies, so that I could ring up the Company if Hewlett turned up at my end, or vice versa. A search had to be made for the H.Q. of the R.E. unit we were attached to. Billy's regiment was passing: I gathered from a brother officer that he was bringing a company up into the trenches that night. I was about an hour looking for these H.Q. and eventually they were somewhere quite different. My ramblings took me through ———,* the mournful wrecks of a village, a street of broken walls, and the road cratered with shell holes. Especially at dusk these places are melancholy, and look as if they might be haunted by strange lonely creatures, Glamis ghosts and the like. The occasional solitary soldier who appears in a broken doorway keeps up the illusion. When I rejoined the Company there was no news. Hewlett had apparently been last seen in the early afternoon and report spoke of heavy shelling in the neighbourhood Our other Company Commander, old ———, had turned up at the appointed place, so I didn't know what to think. Eventually Rogers was found again and proposed that we should help his Company in default of special orders. So we went off with him and drew tools, and we were entering an orchard by a communication trench when a message

* Festubert

came from Hewlett himself, and all was well. The R.E. had failed to send anyone to meet us.

It was a very calm evening where we were ; with the exception of a few bullets that came through the orchard, nothing happened. There was a certain amount of shelling elsewhere and at intervals a searchlight ; that arm of malevolent light appeared at times and lay along the sky line motionless, somehow suggesting the sharks you read of in adventure books dogging a doomed boat. But the beam never came jerking our way. Of our three expeditions it was far the quietest.

Wasn't it luck seeing Vaudrey ? He wrote and arranged a rendezvous and I managed to get off though rather late, and found him in the hotel. Almost exactly a year ago we had gone up to London from Tidworth and spent a happy day, for the ostensible purpose of enrolling ourselves in the U.P.S. A year later the town of meeting was five miles behind the war. He took me to the theatre, a large municipal building out of proportion to the town according to English standards ; the Division stationed round about takes it on, and the Brigade in reserve is expected to supply concerts ; there is also the Divisional band (first-class performances faintly tinged with militarism) and a (very bad) cinema. The troops flock up in regiments and simply love it. Isn't it splendid for them ? It just makes the difference.

Can I have some marking ink ?

JACK

TRENCHES
14th September 1915

DEAR MOTHER

You will notice the change of address. Quite suddenly we were ordered to relieve one of the other brigades. On Sunday afternoon a number of us were summoned to orderly room and when we got there heard the news. Yesterday morning I went on with the Company S.M. along with the other Seconds in Command and their sergeants to spy out the land. We walked the familiar winding road that leads to our trench, through country gradually more militarised and less smiling ... tho' yesterday morning in the breeze and the sunshine, passing along the high road out of which the trenches begin, we might have been holiday makers on a road not wholly given up to the demands of war. I had a happy day, in the character of interested enquirer, among the officers of the company we have relieved. The Company Commander was a mild and easily perturbed old gentleman, who let his Second in Command run the show, doubtless to the advantage of the troops; the rest were the civilians and litterateurs in khaki of the ordinary 1914 stamp. One of them, with his face standing out in the darkness of the dug-out, reminded me absurdly of Armitage. Lunch was a very cheery affair and we bandied memories of Camberley and Clevedon over quite a palatial meal. After that we proceeded to business: the Second in Command took me round and showed me points of interest in the neighbourhood and what to look out for, and answered as many questions as I, bearing in mind Hewlett's forthcoming arrival with the Company and his searching enquiries, could think of to ask. So the day passed very pleasantly. Quite late at night the Company arrived and was shown to its places while the other Regiment filed out. So we were left, no longer attached but really holding the line at last. We are back in a world where all the colours are drab, a world of sandbags and cracking clay, long grass and trees like scare-crows. The dominating colour is dull light brown, with blighted woods showing grey in the background, and between, occasional rows of gaunt trees with broken leafless arms.

Shells have been flying across a certain amount in both directions; the howitzers send them in an arc that leaves you unappalled, until they burst terrifically in the heap of rubble just opposite that was once a farm with hens and homely sights; but shells from the field guns seem to whizz just past your head as if they were bound to graze your parapet on the way. The day has been tedious enough until after tea, when I went out with my platoon sergeant and two good men to reconnoitre. This I enjoyed vastly; we picked up odd scraps of knowledge.

Now that it has been in the papers I can refer to the incident that I spoke of as censored, when I wrote about our first working party. It was after the machine gun had stopped and we were out again carrying on very calmly, when it dawned on my mind in the way unpleasant things do, and this was just the unpleasantest thing that could happen. I was aware of several of the men on the other side of the communication trench we were working at saying " Mr. Ridley," and the name became associated with the word " hit." It was a perfectly clean wound, and our beloved Beatrice is now slowly but surely recovering in Merrie England; but for us it was simply sickening, since Ridley is one of the sweetest souls on earth (tho' O so peevish in the morning), and his removal is the greatest loss to us socially in the Company mess. The men simply adored him. He lay very still and patiently while they bandaged him, and when some hours later on our way home I looked in at the dressing station, he was quite radiant.

I think your Red Cross party must have been splendid and I am so glad you did it.

Good-bye for the present

JACK

TRENCHES
16th September 1915

DEAR MOTHER

It has been so nice receiving letters and parcels. Your letter and Margaret's and the cake came last night. I kept your letter and the cake till the morning, but I had to open something. Mrs. B. is a sportsman; did she ever get a picture post card I sent her? To-night came father's letter and Margaret's parcel, and one I see from Mildred; a long welcome letter from Mr. Dickinson; your "Aunt Sarah and the War," which I have just devoured sitting here in the dug-out, and by which of course I was much struck; and the Galsworthy. I have an idea that I actually asked for the latter; I know I have been wanting it for some time.

You do know of course how much pleasure these letters and parcels give, how they come charged with the thought of the senders.

It is late at night that the post comes and I have put off opening my parcels till the morning. I suppose it is an odd sort of birthday. I thought so this morning, crawling about with my patrol between the trenches. I am at present engaged on a reconnaissance, if such it can be called, that interests and amuses me immensely; each day we have a few more trifling facts and I send in a bulletin. To-day I recognised a piece of it in print, in a sort of news-sheet they issue for certain stretches of the front   Hewlett was away so I was rather busy, but I *am* enjoying this trench life. It was rather curious to read your book describing that man's thoughts of the war; he was enduring that appalling earlier part of it, and we merely having this eminently calm and routiney part.

It is the small hours as I sit in the dug-out lit by a candle in a bottle; I must go out now and see the sentries or I would write further.

Best love to all

JACK

19th September 1915

DEAR MOTHER

The censorship is a perfect nuisance, taking half the flavour out of any letter one writes. Really one can say nothing.

At the moment you would never think the big war was on; the general atmosphere is essentially one of siesta. The September sun burns along the trench, which makes strong shadows here and there like a picture of a narrow street in Southern Europe ; above the sandbags and cracking clay of the parapets is the unbroken blue ; and looking along the trench all you see are the stockinged feet of the soldiery projecting stiffly from the dug-outs. Just occasionally comes the crack of a German sniper's bullet aimed probably at one of our periscopes. The gunners, who usually have a mutual strafe after lunch, are quiet this afternoon.

We followed up my investigations this morning ; Hewlett and I went out this time. It was an absolute picnic, not a Hun to be seen, a breeze and glorious sunshine that filtered through the leaves into the ditch we crawled along. We penetrated quite far and saw all sorts of interesting things, and whispered absurd jokes, and were as happy as kings. I find my pencil very useful. Our part of the line just where the Company is has more points of interest than most in the neighbourhood.

Sometimes passing up and down the line visiting the sentries at unearthly hours, among the grotesque fleeting silhouettes the star-shells make, and hearing the momentary strafes of machine guns at distant suspected targets, or stopping to listen for noises the Germans make working at night, the clink of shovels or a thumping of stakes faintly heard across the wasted fields in a moment of silence, I think how odd it is to be here so occupied.

I had lots of parcels. Margaret's crystallised fruits are excellent, and that and the cake and father's chocolate are greatly appreciated. I love your book and shall enjoy the Galsworthy immensely.

JACK

21st September 1915

DEAR MOTHER

I am so sorry I write short letters nowadays. Things seem somehow to go against writing.

Sunrise to-day was a thing to be remembered. I was going the round then; the long streaks of crimson and purple softened the outlines of this desolate tract, veiling the German lines; above was a great stretch of reddened clouds that flushed our trenches. Against this splendour and mystery a few bursting shells were somehow not an impertinence; and somewhere along the line a thunder of guns, that for days now have been a kind of obbligato to all our doings, was less out of keeping than you would have thought. It was worth being up for.

JACK

I see Varvill is wounded.

23rd September 1915

DEAR MOTHER

Letters must be colourless now-a-days, as the censorship is all agog with its pencil, seeking what it may delete. Otherwise I should tell you heaps of things. How it is, for instance, that Hewlett and I see a great deal of each other in these days, living in a palatial dug-out that belongs at night to the comparatively mighty, and have long and absorbing conversations with a few guns and shells as chorus.*

The *New Statesman* came last night. Very many thanks for the Masefields. In the watches of the

* He and Capt. Hewlett were much engaged on reonnaissance work between the lines at this time.

night I have begun the Galsworthy, from which I get much pleasure.

Hewlett and I divide the night, alternately taking the first and second half of it. One walks, solitary, up and down the trench that the moonlight these last nights has enchanted, turning the dull sandbags to marble. Looking behind you see one of our guns flash and wait for the sound to reach you, wondering whether it will be the rending crash of one fairly near or a more dignified distant rumble. Every now and then we or they send up a light that trails in a graceful arc across, or in front you hear one of our machine guns hammering off a few rounds that echo away into space, or a minute's splutter of rifle fire. Mice scuttle across the trench, and last night a black kitten ran off over the parapet. Sometimes you hear a voice speaking, and remember that besides you and the sentries, a signaller sits through the quiet watches in his lighted dug-out with the receiver to his ear.

The clouds are crowding up this evening as if for a change.

No more now

JACK

TRENCHES
25th September 1915

DEAR MOTHER

The rains are descending and we all wish we had toy boats to sail in the trenches. An Egyptian plague of frogs skips before us as we flounder along. But what of the rain? It can damp our puttees but not our spirits.

Early this morning we saw something of the majesty of war.* I was on duty the first half of the night when all was still, almost ominously so; but at six, sleeping in my dug-out, I became aware of disturbances abroad. These developed into violent whizzes followed by bangs and earthquake effects. Hewlett was just outside and I joined him at the parapet. It was like a conventional presentment of war; a dull dark morning of rain and scudding cloud, and the German lines hidden behind a great drift of smoke streaming earthward, engulfing at times the black timber of a row of withered trees; through it broke red flashes of their guns; behind us were the tremendous explosions of our own, and always the whizzing arched flight of German shells, their burst and rain of bullets. It was altogether without horror, merely most impressive and exhilarating. A few hundred yards off war may certainly have a fine spectacular effect, and of course it was very nice for us to watch, safe behind our parapet.

The rest of the day has been oddly quiet on the whole, and sitting here now we hear only the rain dripping and not a single sound of war. The men take rain jolly well, having fewer conveniences than ever.

I have heard from Arthur and Teddy, birthday letters. Arthur says of course that he won't come back now to quite the home he had dreamed of. Teddy sent a capital letter in his best style.

A shirt or two wouldn't be out of place (not too thick); also an occasional sock.

JACK

* This was the Loos advance

TRENCHES

26th September 1915

Dear Mother

Here I am again at my night vigil, with a brazier of settling embers beside me. Presently I shall go through the "slootch" to the sentries.

I have had a capital post; your cake which will be devoured with enthusiasm to-morrow, or to-day rather, coming as it does after a few days cake-famine; the latest Wells, which is of course extraordinarily welcome (both to Hewlett and myself). Father couldn't have sent anything better; and in the big envelope with the pedantically elegant writing, which you forwarded, some letters of ——, which his brother has had privately printed in Cambridge. They are a voice out of the grave; his whole manner of thought and speech in closest detail are in the printed words; the letters are written to his brother, Mr. Mozley, and others, and are scattered up and down with intimate allusions to Cambridge days and the people of our time there; one or two phrases I recognise that I taught him. One or two are written from England, but most from the trenches and billets in Flanders. To me of course they are extraordinarily vivid.

We have drained our trenches to-day; before there was a Venetian effect, and a system of dams had to be improvised to prevent disastrous flooding of the officers' quarters. The troops don't seem to mind these conditions at all. I have had to pull some of them out of bed to-night to take rations up to one of our companies in the firing line. At two, and it is getting on that way now, I shall call Hewlett, when he will crawl out and carry on while I go to my dug-out, where I have an excellent mattress looted doubtless from a neighbouring ruin.

I have received the *Bystander*, also the battery refills and a letter from father, for all of which many thanks.

I should ask Ridley to stay with you, but he is so shy of meeting people and apparently dislikes visits so much, that he might be very difficult to secure unchaperoned by me.

They won't let him move about for some time yet I think, tho' he is doing well.

I read of the death from wounds of a Pembroke history don, before the War a pacifist, with a large bowl in his rooms the gift of a German pacifist society.

As you see my paper is running out again.

JACK

THE TRENCHES
1st October 1915

DEAR MOTHER
            I haven't forgotten what to-day is the anniversary of. How well I remember that golden afternoon in 1909, when Geoffrey and I came home to a house thronged with aunts and uncles while the Rugby term was in full swing.*

Wednesday was a day of unparalleled wanderings and adventures; you never saw such draggled creatures as we were at the end of it. Now the weather has cleared up again.

* Our Silver-Wedding-Day.

We took over two successive lines in the course of the twenty-four hours, a tremendous feat.

I am so restricted by the censor now-a-days that I never feel quite safe recounting our adventures. At the moment I am sitting on the threshold of the dugout I share with Hughes, hob and nob, owing to the rather bad accommodation just here, and my foot-washing performance is doubtless an amusement to the rude soldiery. My appearance is indescribable in these days, general dirtiness consummating in sacks round my legs while my puttees are being cleaned. I think I wrote for thicker underclothing ; there ought to be some shirts in the luggage I sent home from Tidworth.

While we are in the trenches nothing is so good as sweets in any form, chocolates, acid-drops, peppermint and what-not.

The Colonel's letter about Geoffrey was fine reading.

JACK

POST CARD

4th October 1915

I have just read with infinite sorrow your letter about Billy.* I was fearing to hear of it any day now, knowing that his regiment was in the fighting. I will write later. We are back in civilization again.

JACK

* His cousin, Capt. B. W. E. Hoyle, 9th Welsh Fusiliers, who fell very gallantly at Festubert, September 25th, leading his Company into action.

BILLETS
6th October 1915

DEAR MOTHER

What a noble death was Billy's? But I can't take it in yet.

I do hope that by now you are reassured about me. I can understand how anxious you must have been.

For days we lived on the outskirts of great doings, ready to move; and only the censor kept me from describing the impressions of that time. It was a curious period. Just to the right of us the guns hammered away all day long. I told of how Hewlett woke me one morning to a whizz of shells and the sight of smoke blotting out the German lines. My watch had been the first half of the night before, and I remember sitting in the dug-out and reading in the candle-light the order for the general advance. It struck me at the time as the strangest situation I had ever known; the guns had stopped for the time, and the only sound through the dark hours was the rain dripping from the dug-out roofs. So quiet was it when I went to bed that, in spite of the purport of orders, Hewlett's call seemed a rude awakening. Then the thunder gradually seemed to spend its force to the right of us, and after a period of suspended animation we resumed the normal trench life. A day or two afterwards we went up to the front line trenches again and there stayed very peaceably till the other regiment came to relieve us.

Now we are all going about in clean clothes and uniforms, emerging like butterflies from our case of mud. The first day we were here I had to go to the larger town down the road on a much stranger business, which you shall hear of in due season.

I have received any amount of parcels; the cake, a great success; chocolate and cocoa, always welcome and useful; shirts and socks; refills; the *Bystander* and *New Statesman*; for all of which very many thanks to you and Father. Letters came to-day from you and Margaret. Could you write to Gilbert, he is home now trying for a job in the R.A.M.C.

JACK

OTHER BILLETS
9th October 1915

DEAR MOTHER

We moved a little further up yesterday and are living now in rather broken-down surroundings. The house shakes to our guns. The paper in this room is all peeling off; the furniture is mainly gone, and what's left is bare and cheerless. The four of us sleep like shop assistants in a room four steps up out of this, very comfortably in our valises, with, as it happens, space and convenience to develop our worldly goods in. It is the last strip of habitable country; the houses are intact and people live unconcernedly in them, and the trees are green and happy; but already the gardens are trampled, with rails and planks all about, and end sadly in breastworks and other military devices.

This will be a time of extraordinary impressions when I come to remember it. It was so odd the other day when we were back in the billets we've just left, living a very calm and comparatively luxurious life (I had a capital bed). One morning I had occasion to go up practically into the trenches again like a sort of tourist visiting the war; to begin the day in free and peaceful surroundings and an hour or so after to be warned to beware of snipers; and indeed on the way back some shells burst quite near. There is a stately and beautiful high-road in our area that runs right into the war. Walking along it as I have done several times now, you see the country on one side green and smiling into the distance, with farms and clumps of graceful trees, and on the other the rank grass, dull brown, sprawling everywhere, and in the near distance the scarecrow woods beyond the trenches that you imagine but cannot see.

That morning I saw an officer in our Division who showed me on the map where Billy's regiment advanced. I had met, before we came out, some of his brother officers, and should I see them could get some news. Vaudrey escaped by a miracle; I saw his Adjutant. It is wonderful what your officer said about Billy.

Your sweets and the lavender bag have come; very many thanks.

JACK

12th October 1915

DEAR FATHER

Many thanks for your letters. I quite understand about not being too detailed in describing unpleasant events.* As it happened, your remarks about that came at a time when I had very special reasons for discretion, and my extreme reticence was not the result of your letter.

I hinted the other day at operations. They certainly were rather ludicrous. An advance was due I believe on our right. Anyway we had to obscure our front and confuse the Huns, so we discharged quantities of asphyxiating gas (rather mild as far as I could make out) out of bombs. The order came round rather suddenly and there was no explanation of the move. On went our gas helmets, which of course made us look indescribable. Then at the appointed hour, clouds of smoke began from somewhere lower down and drifted our way. Breathing became less and less pleasant. The wind of course played us false and we were the victims of our own devices. So we stopped and that was all. We expected a frightful strafe in return, but nothing happened, the Germans preserving a grim dignity. Further north I believe we got the wind up on them, and they wasted some ammunition in anxious retaliation. But here I was very shortly afterwards sitting in my observation post basking in the restored October sunshine, in a world apparently at peace.

* The warning was really superfluous. To judge by what we have heard since, his narrative might have been much more thrilling; but, rather than cause uneasiness at home he preferred, as will be seen, to risk appearing humdrum if not trivial.

Hughes, however, lost a finger from a piece of shell that blew back at him and is now on his way to England.

This place is called Glory Hole, and was extremely uncomfortable for everyone concerned a short time back. It is quite harmless now. This morning however they strafed a bit with rather large and very violent shells. Fortunately you hear and see this particular article arriving, and as it has some way to fall from a high trajectory you have time to get out of the way at the sentries' shout. Otherwise they would be most nerve-racking. After an explosion that shakes the immediate neighbourhood, you hear the scattered earth dropping into the trenches round. But the effect is very local. Rifle grenades are our chief terror. You hear them swooping malignantly, but they are tricky to see, and the damage they can do to their victims is remarkable.

I think I must be getting much less sensitive in some directions. I have seen some rather unattractive wounds lately. Last night one of our men had his leg blown right off as far as I could see by one of those things, but I was able to look on without a tremor. I think it will be a comfort to you to know this, as blood used to upset me so much.

I had to accompany the stretcher bearers last night with this particular man. It was an extraordinary journey. Down the long trench we went through the haze of a magical night, serene except for the occasional reports that broke it—a night more fitted for a dance than the business we were engaged in. The man's pluck was quite astonishing.

As long as the weather is fine, as it is now, there is little to complain of in our life out here. I must say I am very happy.

With regard to warm clothing, could I have a trench-coat? A British Warm is hopeless in rain, and a Burberry is inadequate in cold and a snare in rain. When we were caught a few weeks back by the rain and attendant mud, my Burberry was a drawback. I was caked in wet mud far above my knees. (It is a miracle to me that I didn't catch an appalling cold.) But a trench-coat is waterproof and short and lined with most of a sheep or other warm material, which you can take out when required. Do you know the garment?

I received the shirts and am rejoicing in them, though if you send any more, I should prefer a lighter colour. In this statuesque warfare, one has time still to take some interest in such clothes as one is compelled to wear.

I hear from mother that you have been chased by Zeppelins. I am so sorry that you should have worries of that kind added to the mental worries of these times.

JACK

13th October 1915

DEAR MOTHER

I got your letter that came from Brickhill. It is wonderful about Billy. I can't realise that he is gone. It is a great loss to me.

Meanwhile this incredible war goes on. I say incredible because these stationary hostilities are surely the oddest state of affairs man could contrive. One could easily bring one's friends and relations—in small parties—to see the spectacle of conflicting nations (were it not for the military police). One comes and puts in a week or two, carrying the business on, then hands over to someone else and retires to civilisation. I have looked over the parapet sometimes in the dawn and thought how the power and political purpose of Germany is marshalled unseen behind these sandbags across the untented field, and only the fact that one doesn't realise it to the full prevents one from living in a state of continual amazement.

And then what we actually do is so petty. The fate of Europe depends at present on the placing of a sniper's post, over which we spend much anxious thought ; or the discovery, by crawling about with glasses, of a German loop hole ; and other small things quite out of keeping with the importance of the interests involved.

However it is great fun, and I for one am very happy. We are in a most notorious spot just now, the sort of place that a few weeks back we whispered of and shuddered. It has turned out quite harmless, the Germans having possibly discovered that our guns, as they usually do now, give them back good interest for the bombs and other contrivances they send over.

We are lucky in having a spacious mess just built by the R.E. which you enter from a flight of steps. There is a wooden seat running round and a movable table in the middle. We entertain Artillery Officers just now, which of course is delightful socially, and we can also lay deep schemes together for the destruction of Prussian influences in Europe.

I had a charming letter from Varvill, who is now back in Nottingham, recovering from wounds he got in the Dardanelles. His eyes, he says, were bunged up by a high explosive. He was a week in Malta on the way back, and when in hospital in London was attended to by a lady in shrimping costume.

Love to all
JACK

20th October 1915

DEAR MOTHER

I am so sorry that you shouldn't have heard from me for some days; but I dare say you will have done by now. I wrote a line almost every day we were in the trenches.

Truly these are stirring times. I have had quite a typical day. Last night we reached the slightly broken down billets we left for the Glory Hole. The order came round later that we were to send a working party on the morrow, and it was my turn to take it. Accordingly I rose at six and had an early breakfast alone, and then led my small band out through the still morning. After sailing calmly out of the danger zone the night before, and returning to billets amid cheery shouts by the men of "bomb up," it was curious to return to it in the morning. We reached an orchard which is an important R.E. railway centre, and waited for our guide and for material to arrive by trolley. It was a cheerful scene in the misty October light, the orchard having preserved its youth and beauty quite remarkably in spite of rails and revetments. The place was full of R.E., moving planks and riding on trucks they were shunting. We got our job at last and went up to the front line. I was settling down to the prospect of the day's work when to my amazement, Johnson, the Canadian who has now joined us from C Company, came hustling up announcing that he was relieving me as I had to go to a court-martial at Brigade H.Q. Down I went full speed, being already an hour over-due, found the bike Johnson had left for me on the main road and rode away, leaving the war further behind. I had to wait a long time at Brigade H.Q. as there were several cases to get through. It is a fine big farm standing back from the road, and the offices are the ghosts of the stately rooms. Sewell and I talked with the Staff Captain (once our Adjutant) until I heard that my case wouldn't come on till after lunch. Coming away we met the Brigade Signalling Officer, tall and slim and cultured in stockings and brogue shoes, leaning gracefully on a long pole. He suggested a walking tour in the decorative style. He treated us to five minutes manierè conversation, and with Sewell to answer, (do you remember him with Vellacott that Sunday at the Tidworth Club ?) you can imagine there was little need for me to speak. When I reached my billet, eager for lunch, I found the place swept and garnished, and a multitude of little slouch-hatted Indians squatting and jabbering in the orchard. To my amazement we had had sudden orders to move to fresh billets half-a-mile further from the war. I had time to make a few arrangements and pack my Platoon off, and then broke away from them at the corner and returned to the Brigade Office. I found the Brigade Transport Officer and asked for lunch ; there was some demur and the suggestion of a surreptitious meal in the back-ground, but shortly I was ushered into the Presence. So after the adventures of the morning I found myself sitting up with the gilded Staff at a large table spread with a cloth and cut glass. The General was very friendly. Then I had a rather boring afternoon on my unpleasant business, standing about in the cold. It ended at last and I went in search of the new billets. I found the men installed in fine barns with lots of straw. We, the officers, were supposed to inhabit dug-outs, but during the afternoon Hewlett had found room for us in farms. So Johnson and I sleep on the floor in this room (a valise with straw in and a sleeping bag make a capital bed), and Hewlett elsewhere.

Since beginning this one night elapses. Johnson took the working party this morning. The Brigadier inspected each company in turn. He was in high spirits, and announced that the Regiment had now made a name that needed keeping up.

The family really has had adventures. Father gave me a full account of his misfortune at Euston. It was cruel.

I can imagine that the scenery you describe was beautiful. The country here is as flat as a billiard table ; ploughed land with beans on poles and dotted with farms ; everywhere are exquisite Corot vignettes in the delicate misted October sunshine. I met one of our officers to-day who spoke of Billy, having seen him at that course at Perham Down ; he said that he looked every inch a gentleman and that everyone said so.

We are getting another officer, which is all to the good. Little Hughes lost a finger the other day while using his periscope in our grand demonstration, and will now be back in Holland Park pursued by a mess bill from me.

Perry left us weeks ago with appendicitis, and Hewlett and I are the only ones left of the old guard.

If our programme holds good your mind may be at rest for some little time now.

Teddy must be really happy.

JACK

I had a note from Ridley. The creature, as I suspected, doesn't care a rap what happens to us now. Have you written yet? I will tell him to visit you in my answer.

23rd October 1915

DEAR MOTHER

I have received the cake and sweets, for which many thanks.

It is beautiful October weather, very misty and cold in the earlier morning, and the sun gradually filters through with very delicate effect on the turning leaves.

I took the company's working party yesterday, but this morning lay in my valise and watched Johnson pull himself together. Our new officer declares he comes from the Civil Service, but is vague when questioned further and something about him suggests that Civil Service is an elastic term, like Public Schools.

We live now on the edge of the stately Rue —— [1] (the main road between —— [2] and —— [3]) which I have quite an affection for now. From the far side of it come noises of the war, a machine gun hammering a few rounds off, and low rumbling crashes of the guns. In peace time it must be a charming spot, but the continual sojourns and migrations of the troops through the months have done for it more or less, and the vines hang tangled from the walls. It is extraordinary to think that had I chosen to-day I could have ambled up to the war as an afternoon's stroll, an entirely irresponsible person, and had a real look at it and talked with officers actually engaged in carrying it on, and then come back to tea.

Your loving son

JACK

24th October 1915

DEAR MOTHER

We are back now in the billets of those quite distant days when we sent out our first working parties and Ridley was wounded. So you can rejoice and divide Succoth. I have found a very nice little room for myself in a clean farm.

I have received the cake, the handkerchiefs, underclothing and socks. For all, our thanks. Will you also thank Father very much for the cigarettes which are excellent, and for the fountain pen.

[1] Rue du Bois   [2] Bethune   [3] Neuve Chapelle

I haven't seen a paper for days, tho' I was much stimulated by Garvin's exposition in last week's Observer, in which he turns our attention to the Serbia business. Do you see his weekly articles? They are quite Periclean utterances.

No more for the present

JACK

*Teddy must be rejoicing, tho' you will feel anxious.

*His sailor brother had just put to sea in command of H.M.S. *Azalea* Mine-Sweeper.

26th October 1915

DEAR MARGARET

I have read your long letters with the greatest pleasure, though they have not been acknowledged as they should.

Your Zeppelin experiences were thrilling reading, but I do think that sort of thing is hard on people who have the mental sufferings of the War to bear. Out here, where it is a case of bombs, there is a certain humour in dodging them, but at home there can be little mental background for such amusements.

Even yet I have hardly realized how much Billy's death means, or the loss, to me among others. It seems too cruel that the War should claim such a victim, and those hands that played the piano so beautifully. The thought comes in what splendid music Vergil would have mourned so fair a promise cut short, comparing the shattered soldier to a blossom gathered in a careless moment and thrown aside, and one recalls too the rhythms of Lycidas.

I had a sweet letter from Aunt Zöe.

France is lovely this Autumn, and now that we are out of the firing line there is time and opportunity to enjoy it. This country abounds in groups and rows of exquisite trees standing round about their graceful farms, and turning the corner of a lane you come continually on little pictures that seem to belie the reality of War.

I must stop for the present.

JACK

The following letter was written after his first home leave.

7*th November* 1915

DEAR MOTHER

Back to the Army again; and not so bad either.

When I had posted my letter of yesterday morning I had a jolly bus-ride into the Belgravia world and went to the Pitmans'. I was shown into a dream of a drawing room, all in exquisite greys and very homely at the same time. The interview was a matter of messages, with the parlour-maid as medium, as Mme. Hilda was indisposed, but I left with her blessing. She managed to convey a divine effect of Homer's Helen, by practically nothing at all.

The platform at Victoria was crowded with officers in all rigs, and fine men and courageous women. I found Bell immediately and we both said how splendid it had all been. There could have been no better send-off than the loveliness of Kent. And is not Kent called the " Garden of England?" I had never dreamed it half so beautiful.

A dirigible was manœuvring very decorously over the cliffs as we waited on the quay. Luckily I wasn't landed with a platoon of ruffians to look after. We left of course in broad daylight. After all there is a certain dignity in these daily silent departures. The boat slips out of harbour and the escort picks her up, and from the grey receding quay there is no sadness of farewell. Only one knows what is felt in the quiet land behind.

It was an entirely uneventful crossing. The spirit of it was of course far different from last time. Then it was the first stage of a Homeric adventure; and now it seemed the most natural thing in the world to be gliding in among the lights between the high walls of the fort, and hear the foreign shouts and an officer with a megaphone giving directions and calling out names.

There followed a long search among the lines and coaches for the right train, amid the babel of queries and the solicitations of women with fruit and chocolate. We chose one in the end and started at about 7-30. We all slept pretty well in the train. (The Quarter Master had joined us by this time, also old Sankey, of Warrington). When the train reached *——— somewhere about three o'clock I suppose, we decided to get out there, as the walk to †——— would be shorter than

* Bethune † Locon

from our original station of departure. The station at *—— was rather cheerless it must be confessed. It was odd to be going through the town in darkness that made the streets unfamiliar, shouting to each other about our way. The walk to billets was rather jolly. Away to the right came an occasional thud—the War again—but the few guns that fired sounded unusually quiet, as if the "autumn dripping death dumb night" had taken the heart out of them. Cocks however were crowing in the farms we passed. I left my bag eventually with a sentry and the defaulters were sent to fetch it to-day. It was about half-past four when I crept into the little farm where I sleep. My servant had got all ready.

Hewlett (who is shocked beyond measure at my cap) let me off church parade, to settle the mess accounts. France too looked lovely this afternoon in the November sun.

Please delay the despatch of the peppermint and creme de menthe by a week.

I have read "Daddy Long Legs" and of course was delighted. I thought it very clever, as well as charming.

I hope the meeting on Friday morning was a success.

JACK.

* Bethune

11th November 1915

DEAR MOTHER

I am afraid there will have been a gap in my letters, but time has been rather full.

We are back in the trenches again, in a desolation of mud indescribable, but I plunge through it immune, safe in the waders Winser sold me. The men too are in similar garb. My appearance is, according to Hewlett, indescribable, in Engadine cap (not let down), trench coat (which is fine), and the waders.

It took no time to settle down again. Before I went on leave the thought of a dismal return cast a shadow across the most joyous anticipations; but I re-entered the scenery of *—— without a pang, and leave has become a set of delightful memories. Indeed it was wonderful.

Sunday was very quiet and soothing. On Monday Johnson and I brought a working party up here; I have never seen such mud. I walked on top all the time to avoid it, and the Germans made no observations. They did though later, and, while I was in the front line with Gibson of Magdalen, sent some shells right where the party was; but we retaliated and their batteries were rapidly silenced.

We moved in here last night. ——† is immediately behind. The Hun is very quiet and there is no "trench warfare" as far as we are concerned. Our chief job at present is to repair dug-outs. To-morrow we begin a series of working parties. Fortunately the rain is intermittent and we have seen quite a lot of the sun to-day.

JACK

*Locon   †Festubert

13th November 1915

DEAR MOTHER

I wrote my last one night after the post had gone and I wasn't there to despatch it the next day, so I'm afraid you'll have been waiting for news.

These days have been pretty strenuous. They left us alone our first day in the trenches, and we had time to do some very necessary repairs to the roofs of the dug-outs. My waders protected me from such mud and water as there was. The mess was quite comfortable, except that you had to squeeze yourself in through a rabbit-hole entrance. On the next day I took a working party up to the front line. It took an incredible time wading up there through the mud, which was in places over one's knees. The return journey was worse if anything, and it was dark when we straggled in, having abandoned one pair of thigh boots belonging to a hapless fellow who had to be dug out by his friends.

Yesterday we got the order to move into *—— for the night, and move back into another part of the line next day. There is a road still in good condition that runs out of *—— right into the trenches where we were, and I went down there in the afternoon to have a look at the houses we were to inhabit. The accommodation was not tempting, as very few roofs were anywhere near complete, and water drips through on to the accumulated rubble and old clothes and scattered paper underneath. An officer of B was living in a good dug-out in the remains of the church. It is curious to see this ghost of a village; the shell of everything is still here. By the shreds of wall paper and the tiles that

* Festubert

remain, the house we have taken as H.Q. was one of the better class. The mess cook (the ex-chauffeur) soon rigged up a fire, and last night, perched on anything handy in the draughty tumbled barracks of a room that had lost its ceiling, we had our regular dinner exactly the same as always. Hewlett and I have got a corner to sleep in that is better than most. Some of the men had a wretched night. At present we are hanging about waiting for orders, as the details of relieving just here are very complex. At this most inconvenient hour large consignments of boots and socks have arrived for issue.

JACK

BRITISH ARMY IN THE FIELD
FRANCE
19th November 1915

DEAR MOTHER

As the men say, "I now take the pleasure of writing you these few lines hoping that it will find you as it leaves me in the pink at present."

We are now settling down to the winter campaign, and the chief impression is mud, "slootch." It pervades all our quarters, and we have become quite shameless (tho' emphatically not as bad as a certain other regiment who threw up the sponge much earlier).

After our strange sojourn in *——, where we lay like conies among the rocks, we came back the next day to a slightly different part of the line. I went up

* Festubert

in the afternoon to spy out the land, and found the above regiment keeping up the tradition. The officers were in a sort of coop where they sat all day, indescribably dirty and unshaved, with their bootless feet in sandbags, and waited for orders and food to be shovelled at them. When we took over that part we were up and doing all the time, and we did shave and dabble our hands in biscuit boxes. There was a certain amount of bickering the first night with the Headquarters Staff who appeared to encroach on our line ; one found coveted dug-outs occupied by the Regimental Sergeant-Major or his myrmidons, who seemed to rise up from the ground. I had secured a place for Johnson in the afternoon ; Hewlett and I slept in the coop. On the whole it was what we call "hopeless dawn" next morning. It was something of a blow to see looming up an officer from D, attached to us. We call him Minenwerfer, which is a corruption of his name. There was no mess accommodation, so we had our meals perched on dug-out roofs quite happily. The sun shone and we made various improvements, including a dug-out for myself, so that Hewlett might possess the coop undisturbed, a much better arrangement for both. At lunch time I had a message from Orderly Room telling me to report in the afternoon to one of the batteries of the Divisional gunners, and to spend the night. Thus doubtless it is thought to promote co-operation. So off I went in the afternoon and found a very friendly, rather (as Hewlett suggested) "Richmond cum-Twickenham" R.F.A. subaltern at the appointed ruin. Horses were waiting at a bend in the road. I mounted with considerable difficulty, stuffed up as I was in equipment and trench coat, and wearing thigh boots. Down a long avenue of tall trees we went towards the misted greys and carmines of sunset, cautiously for the shell holes in the roads; then, emerging from a waste of sandbagged ruins and water-logged disused trenches, we quickened the pace as the lights shone in the windows and the roads were better. We pulled up eventually at the Battery billet, a farm where they all live with their guns round them. We found another equally friendly gunner subaltern in the parlour, a burly Irishman whom I liked very much. It was an almost tumultuous welcome, with a great deal of "dear old boy," especially from the Richmondy one. Less conspicuous was an anti-aircraft subaltern of a more refined public school type. His name was Denham; and it transpired that he was at Balliol and loved Billy as his dearest friend, saying he would never have such another. We parted with exchanged addresses.

There followed of course a very sociable and enjoyable evening, with a hot bath and dry clothes (I wore artillery badges), fresh interests and fresh conversation. It was thrilling to listen to another aspect of the war. We had a long talk, rather seditious in places, to the disadvantage of a certain branch of the army. We talked of the 25th, and I tried to pick up all I could, but there was little new. I woke up next morning to the shouts of the troops in the orchard; they were making a dug-out for the signallers and kept breaking off to chase startled rats. It was a gay scene in the still graceful orchard fresh with morning sun; everybody seemed to be in highest spirits except perhaps the signaller at the telephone, who must have been cold, and whose persistent and doleful "hello" suggested broken communication. After breakfast I went with my first host (the stalwart Moriarty being by that time at his observing station) round the demesne and inspected a gun and shells, feeling like an amiable M.P. being shown manœuvres. Then for my benefit they did "battery action," and fired several times at some ruin behind the enemy trenches; we stood in the gun-shed part of the time, and I am glad to say that my ears weren't *"sharpened," tho' I almost thought they would give way. But the great thing is to have your mouth open, otherwise it is like stopping a fast cricket ball with a stiff arm or jumping off a wall on to your heels. Then I dressed for the road, as Arthur says, and having parted with the friendly Hull, ambled on a most unambitious horse with a chatty and unmilitary orderly to the furthest point you can ride to. It was a perfect morning and even the desolate land looked fair; arched over rather a pretty ruin was a weeping willow still as green as summer, that brought a sudden illusion of The Backs. In a street of ruins leading out of † I found Moriarty, who seeing me coming afar off, rather fat and waddly in trench coat and waders, had taken me for some important and middle-aged officer. Then I had a vastly interesting time. We climbed up improvised stairways to the top of a ruined house, and looked through the telescope at the two lines of trenches, while I was shown landmarks for the gunners and their positions on the map. I would have stayed there for hours and made sketches of the whole, but it was time to rejoin the Company. Altogether it was a delightful interlude.

* He was always extremely sensitive to sound. We have a very vivid memory of him on a railway platform as a small child, his agonized expression as he vainly tried to shut out the scream of the engine whistles and his lament "it sharpens my ears."

† Givenchy.

I found that the Company had orders to move up to the front line that evening. The which we did. The front line is perfectly astonishing, tho' I must not say why. That was as weird a twenty-four hours as I ever remember. The scene suggested collapse and desolation indescribable. We got the men somehow into their places, feeling vaguely responsible for bringing them into such comfortless quarters. Each little party was marooned amid a waste of mud and water; the moon's reflection shook in the flooded deserted trenches. There was a vast silence as if both armies were stupefied by their surroundings. Only the moon and the "tingling stars" testified to the ancient order of things. We seemed to be in a salient, that might have been a jumping-off-place at the limit of the world; beyond our tumbled moonlit sandbags was a shimmering tract blotched with dark shell holes; the flares that swam noiselessly up from behind the opposite parapet, and the occasional shots, and the short bursts of their machine guns did not in the least detract from the utter loneliness and silence. Absurdly crowning it all, we heard a flight of strange unseen birds, that flew over with grating cries such as I have never heard. For a time we thought it was some German device.

Minenwerfer was maroooned away to the right. Hewlett, Johnson and I crowded into a small wooden shelter near the centre of the line. We brought in quantities of mud with us. It was my tour of duty from twelve to four. When I turned out the weather had changed; the stars were gone and it was a night of scudding cloud and mist and cold wind, as if blowing up for rain. For hours I stumbled about that forlorn region, doing the hearty when I came upon sentries, (so as to warm them up I made some of them run about above ground, to their apparent reluctance). Flares would steal up from the German lines, turning the mist dull yellow, and then slowly dropping as they lighted up; at such times the German trenches were a dark formless bank against the wan mist. I reached our extreme right, where a sentry of the next Division, hearing my gropings, challenged in an absurdly loud rather comic voice of no particular dialect, tho' his county is famous for its burr. Just as my tour was ending, I slipped into the trench, and after some fruitless struggles I felt the water gurgling in over the top of my boots. Fortunately I had some rum in the flask you gave me, and there were no ill effects.

I was entirely confined next day to the dug-out while my socks were drying; bnt the others had only about twenty yards they could move in, and for most of the time we three lay in our hutch, reading and talking, and laughing at the absurdity of our situation. At intervals the servants shovelled meals at us. It was an odd day. The *Sporting and Dramatic* was invaluable. So was Masefield's "Street of To-day," which we had telephoned for weeks before, during the great advance, to the fury of the Brigade Office.

Happily the rain did not come. By tea-time my socks were dry, and I got out and scrambled eggs for the party. In the evening we went down to the next line further back. Here the mud was terrific but negotiable. Here too was the ghost of a proper mess with a capital bedroom opening out; only the floor of the latter was six inches under water. However Hewlett and I slept on raised beds. There followed a day of sploshing about looking after the men, and in the evening back we went to this line again. In our previous stay I had built a dug-out for myself, with an excellent if rather bibulous-looking Irish old soldier as foreman. Owing to the artillery stunt I couldn't test it that time, but last night I returned to it with the feeling of a Roman litterateur returning to his villa in the country.

We woke up this morning to a world white with frost, dry and very jolly when you had conquered the cold, which didn't take long. (In this connection could I have some device for feet at night, as very thick woolly socks or some kind of bag?).

It has been a happy day in spite of the thaw, and we are comparatively clean again. Comparatively of course. I really must stop now.

Very many thanks for cakes, papers, &c. Tell Father the trench coat is splendid, tho' alas, what a breaking-in it and Brigden's latest effort have had.

JACK

Nov. 19. Civilisation again to-morrow night.

Under the category of sweets, chocolates like Velma are always delectable.

Can I have a copy of the "Child's Garden of Verses," or anything else really R.L.S., such as "Vailima Letters"?

25th November 1915

DEAR MOTHER

Let me begin by denying authoritatively—is that the correct Press Bureau and Asquith formula?—any such upheaval of our plans as you took the changed address to mean. I was quite horrified by Father's suggestion. We do however know who are the people involved.

It transpires too that the new address is not after all a definite order. I was told it immediately on my return from leave, but I have only just found that it hasn't appeared in orders.

It is many days since I sent home a detailed despatch. The last was written just before we went up for our second dose of the front line. It all seemed more commonplace this time, and certain improvements had been made. Hewlett lived with Minenwerfer on the right, while Johnson and I were marooned with our respective platoons, I inhabiting our old haunt. I was up all that night wandering round and doing odd things. With some difficulty we found coils of unused wire, then I collected a few men and we went out and made entanglements, rather amateurishly, but it was quite fun. It was bright moonlight and we were an odd group; a reel of barbed wire is an awkward instrument for the unpractised, and we were almost caught like the heathen in the net we laid.

I never told you that all the ground we held that week was the very place where Billy's regiment advanced; our wire was shot to pieces and tangled up.

I wanted to go out on patrol and see what the Germans were doing, but the moon was so very bright I didn't think we could get anywhere. But about five in the morning clouds came up, so I seized my grimmest lance-corporal and out we crawled. There was a cold morning wind stirring, in the right direction for us. We reached at one point a ditch which had to be crossed gingerly so as not to make the ice clink too loud. It was a desolate scene—just a waste of blown dull-coloured grass (I recognised on the way back the ghost of some corn) with a few leafless scraggy shrubs by the frozen ditch, and always in my mind the thought that here was that terrible advance. Eventually we had to turn back, like Richard I. from Jerusalem, without reaching their wire, lest daylight should catch us out there. There were continual cheery shouts in the German lines and singing, but I couldn't make anything out.

The day passed placidly enough, except that just at the end the lance-corporal I had been out with that morning got wounded—very nicely and safely—but I am sorry to lose him. In wading to the place where he was, to bring him in, the mud and water came pouring over my gum-boots, which was a bit trying, but as I had plenty of walking about to do I didn't feel the cold. Then in the evening the other regiment came up to relieve us, and out we trekked through a winter night of extraordinary beauty among the ruins of *————, to a house where we took off our waders and got into ordinary boots, which felt very nice again. I had, too, dry socks. People wriggled out of their waders with some difficulty and then off we went—away from it all. Never had a room looked so pleasing as our headquarters mess in

*Festubert

that billet; it was a grade higher than any we have had yet, and one got an impression of a lighted fireplace with a big mirror and cream-coloured panelled walls, all in the comfortable light of a candle on the round polished table. Daylight rather dispelled this and other illusions about the farm where Johnson and I were; but about my valise there was no doubt.

The next day was spent in making various preparations for the move on Monday. I took some men to the Brigade Office to change their boots. It was as picturesque a place as you could wish to see. You went through an archway into a cobbled yard with out-houses all round, and at the end, reached by steps, the house, quaint and tall and dominating.

Monday was bright and beautiful and frosty, and as I said was like coming home for the Christmas holidays. The place is full of memories. This is the same orchard where we basked on drowsy August afternoons and had our dinner by flickering candlelight under the trees. Ridley too, a blue-eyed pastoral figure, graced the scene very appropriately. Hughes and Perry are gone, giving place to Johnson and Minenwerfer.

The weather is beautiful, and the country is looking as pretty as it did in the summer.

We are going back to a sort of Clevedon or Andover period of training and the war might be miles away. We do just hear a gun or two occasionally and the flares at night look quite near.

To-day it is snowing.

JACK

27th November 1915

DEAR MOTHER

Parcels have arrived to-day containing night-socks from you and Father, also chocolate and the camel-hair waistcoat. Very many thanks. The last cake too was excellent.

Life is going pretty calmly now. There was a contretemps though the second night, in the form of a chit to us from Orderly Room to the effect that the successors in our billets of Sunday had complained that we had left the place dirty, so the Brigadier directed us to send parties back to clean up. It was a blow for Hewlett of course (B Company shared our disgrace). I was detailed to take our party, and you can imagine it was an ignominious affair unravelling those eight miles we had marched so triumphantly a day or two before. One of the men said the——shires (who had made the complaint) must be a ——Lord Mayor's show. We knew of course that the greater part of the mess was made by our numerous predecessors.

As we arrived there was a terrific report from a heavy gun they had brought up; cart-horses reared and a window fell into the road incontinent. We reached our billet and proceeded to eat humble pie. The regiment in question had gone, giving place to some units of the Old Army, with faultless colour-sergeants, who stiffened into alert statues at one's approach. The officers though are mostly New; and these, as often, were bent on your quite understanding that theirs is one of the Old Divisions, while the number of yours is something unthinkable. The Company Commander recalled a Cambridge rowing Blue, and would have been quite a nice creature had not belonging to a Regular battalion been rather too much for him. He was very haughty at first. I set the men cleaning up, which they did rather well, scavengering the refuse of countless previous occupants. Later the Captain unbent sufficiently to give me lunch. It was only fair to say they had made the mess extremely untidy. We lunched to a gramophone accompaniment, which was cheerful. It was dark when we finally got back, all rather tired. I found the C.O. and Adjutant on my return in here and Hewlett and I were asked to dinner. I felt bound to accept, though I should have preferred early bed. However it was a very cheery affair, quite like old days. Sewell and Sankey were there from D, and there was quite a crowd round the long table at H.Q. The C.O. was quite hilarious, and all went merrily.

This morning we took our platoons to have baths in a neighbouring town; this is always a popular show. In the afternoon the football and pump were used.

I have had two pleasant meetings lately. The morning before we went up to the front line, who should come along in the wake of the Brigade Signalling Officer but Morshead of Magdalene, one of the most charming people in the world; you may remember him at tea in Salter's rooms. And as we were marching out on the Monday I found another Magdalene acquaintance at the tail of one of the Companies relieving us. At these meetings one steps for a moment into another world.

JACK

The other day they sent round to say that Mrs. Winser and Mrs. Vellacott were arranging to send plum puddings to the soldiery, with the hoped-for assistance of officers' relations, and would we give names. So I put you down and you will probably hear of it shortly.

1st December 1915

DEAR MOTHER

Many thanks for the gloves; the tape is rather long, but that can easily be remedied.

Will you tell Father that the surmises in his letter of the 28th with regard to our occupation are quite correct, that being just the information I should have given had I been indiscreet.

There is a general harlequinade going on at present, all the officers doing various unexpected jobs. Sewell will soon be a member of the gilded Staff. For myself I am aspiring to be Signalling Officer. I was offered the job a few days back and refused it, and then cursed myself bitterly for losing the chance; so I asked if I could reconsider my decision; found that I had disappointed and offended the C.O., but was allowed to try my hand.

So now every morning I repair to Brigade Headquarters and seek out the Brigade Signalling Officer. He had just finished three years at Oxford when the war broke out, got out to France immediately, went through some of the Mons business, came home and stayed there till he came out again with the Division. Meeting him is just like going into someone's rooms at the Varsity. Every morning we go into the town to get cash for troops, he imparting knowledge all the time, I interrupting occasionally like a disciple of Socrates. About the grounds of Headquarters we often meet Koster walking round with Sewell as his pupil in exactly the same way. Koster has got a pretty big rise and is teaching Sewell to walk in his shoes.

In the afternoon I go to Battalion Orderly Room and receive further instructions from Vellacott, who is training me to know his work in case of emergency. It is office work, consisting so far of my writing letters to important officials at the base, or stuffy notes to Company Commanders, for his signature.

The last cake is having a succés fou. I was delighted to get the Stevenson.

JACK

5th December 1915

DEAR MOTHER

We are on trek again, contrary to expectations. To-morrow night may see us in the trenches. It was a surprise, and we are sorry at the sudden end of our Christmas Holidays, but there is nothing alarming in the reason for it, which is very hum-drum.

Two mornings ago I came on to early parade at *—— and found the troops not in the dress they had been ordered to wear for the Brigadier's inspection. I sent them back to put it on, faintly surprised at their incredulity, and learned that orders had come through in the small hours for an immediate move   I was

*Merville

detailed to go ahead and do the billeting. At the Brigade Office the greatest excitement prevailed. The general was pacing up and down and the Staff were grimly active, Sewell intent on the unlooked for development of his new duties. We were to drive over there in the car. As we crossed the graceful iron bridge a swan was gliding up the moat with languid pulses. To the right stood a house on its mound, looking suddenly the very embodiment of peace and civilized life, against the mud and sandbags of our anticipation. Driving through the streets was like driving through the City, so full were they of morning traffic.

We arrived at the village of our quest and I was dumped at the centre of the battalion area. Then followed the real billeting nightmare of rushing about amid already crammed billets, with the regiment every moment coming nearer. It was of course comic, but rather desperate too. Up and down the village I went, in and out of farms, with the same old formula, occasionally scraping up an odd billet, and endeavouring to melt the women with elaborate pronunciation and pathetic tones. At last I went to a more remote spot, and to my rapture was told at the first farm, which welcomed me openly, that there were no troops in the neighbourhood. After that of course I got billets like wild-fire comparatively, the only drawback being the thought that the regiment had by this time—and they were more than due—arrived at ———, and were unanimously fuming as they waited. I found them on my return, but they had only been there a few minutes and my reception was reassuring, the difficulties being apparently understood. I was given a horse (which I mounted far from gracefully) and was able to rush about and show Company Commanders the way. One senior officer was rather stuffy, but all the others were tremendous sportsmen. Very little happened for the rest of the day, or on the next. This morning we moved again. One officer went from each company to take our billets. We left early in the morning. The tide roads are under water, which my horse didn't like particularly. We passed through *—— with its chapel of almost Saxon date, full of reminiscences of August days. We found the billets in very decent ruins near †—— and returned to pick up our companies, who were long in coming. I seem to have been riding all day, as, after having brought the troops, alone I went back to find our wagon with the blankets.

So here we are in a waste land again, among fields run wild and near the jumping lights. It is not cold, and we have the best reports of this particular line and are quite happy. The men are just overhead, singing lustily.

JACK

* Vieille Chapelle   †Neuve Chapelle

9th December 1915

DEAR MOTHER

Just a line. We are in the trenches and quite happy, tho' the mud is exasperating. Please send candles; sweets of all sorts and any dainties would meet an increasing demand. I enclose the letter about Geoffrey which is splendid.

JACK

10th December 1915

DEAR MOTHER

I confess that when I wrote that note yesterday the mud and wet had momentarily got the better of me, and I was feeling irritated and depressed. To-day, tho' the mud is worse if anything, my mind is at peace with the world.

We left our ruins on Wednesday. The Company had two cottages. We inhabited two rooms of one, with the servants in the kitchen, and half the men very noisily overhead. We were as civilised as the circumstances allowed.

On the Tuesday night I brought a working party up here. We were once more on historic ground, as the ruins of *—— are just to the left. It was very quiet. An ex-Magdelenite, supported by two unattractive subordinates, commanded the company in occupation. As usual they had given up all thought of keeping clean. The wet certainly did not help matters. You sit with your feet in a kind of trough; the kitchen is a sort of cave leading out of it through an irregular hole in the wall; here the scullion sits and hands things through. However I was given supper, so there was nothing to complain of.

On the Wednesday afternoon I came up to prepare the way. A corporal had cut me a vast pole, which was a great comfort. It had been a day of exquisite beauty that made even this forlorn country seem to smile ; as I came up a road that runs right into the front line, shafts of the declining sun beat on the ghosts of walls and touched them to glory.

* Neuve Chapelle.

Major Monteagle B———, Second in Command of the ———, lived in a superb dug-out in the reserve line. This stood a little back and had windows like an office, through which I could see him sitting as at the receipt of custom. He is an opulent and comfortable person and looked very quaint. Hewlett decided to take over his quarters, and I, later, changed my mind and found a place down there instead of up here, so that it is more comfortable for all of us. My place was a bit leaky last night so I went into Hewlett's, which has two berths like a stateroom in a ship; we had, too, a roaring fire in a brazier and were able to dry our clothes. My platoon lives in a kind of warren across the way, and comes up here by day for work in the front line. It is a very amusing life; the Hun has almost ceased from troubling, tho' our guns must try him a little at intervals. The weather is very mild though inclined to wet.

Many thanks for the towel and cake, &c. I hope the plum-pudding scheme will eventuate; I imagine you have heard nothing more about it.

We took part in quite grotesquely absurd operations yesterday, tho' I must not describe them.

Excuse my clamour for sweets. You can't think what a solace they are. Anything like crystallised ginger, chocolate, biscuits, &c., are received with avidity.

JACK

The letter about Geoffrey *is* splendid. It sounds true.

11th December 1915

DEAR MOTHER

I loved your description of the Billiard Room, "The War and Women" scene. Many thanks in anticipation for the F. & M. box.

Life here continues very pleasantly. The trough mess, after the night's rain, was voted quite intolerable at breakfast time, and we have removed the mess root and branch to the better quarters where the Monteagle was discovered, a far better arrangement. It was "hopeless dawn" again this morning. I had the watch from four to eight, and day broke drearily with piles of driving cloud. It has cleared up since and there has been real sunshine. I have moved my sleeping quarters as the place next to Hewlett's leaked. Grubbing about in that sort of deserted city down there I found a dry dug-out with a real bed. My servant made a wood fire which set the shadows jumping, and reading the Stevenson letters by my candle before I turned in I was very snug and happy, and having the bed was quite rested when Johnson called me in the small hours.

Old Minenwerfer is turning out well and his heavy manner becomes quite amusing. You will be pleased to hear that an officer has recently joined who is not a social problem, tho' unfortunately he is posted to another company.

Our sudden return to the war put the lid on my signalling and other activities, for the time at any rate, tho' Vellacott called me in to take his place one morning in the ruins when he was away. No, I hadn't actually got the appointment, but was on trial. Also Vellacott likes training other folk to take his place in case of emergencies, wherein I think he is wise.

This morning I saw the first Hun I have yet clapped eyes on. He was sniping, but not at us. Our own sniper claims to have got him this afternoon.

JACK

Candles are urgent ; also the cape I asked for.

13th December 1915

DEAR MOTHER
    A line to say that we left the trenches last night and returned to our ruins, which seemed like home. We decorated the room with licentious and cheery pictures from the Christmas Sketch, and our evening meal, to a roaring fire, was capital. Unexpectedly this morning we moved again to another set of deserted houses.

It is beautiful weather.

JACK

15th December 1915

DEAR MOTHER
    Your Christmas parcel came last evening. I imagine that the remark on the wrapper did not mean that it wasn't to be opened yet; an unopened parcel might be an awkward thing in this life. I was simply delighted with the presents; handkerchiefs are always welcome, and the shoes are absolutely first-rate; the most soothing things you could have sent—a blessing in the morning and "at the close of day, possibly sweetest."

We are enjoying our battalion rest, even tho' the surroundings are extraordinary. A war makes wonderful changes in one's values; a bare room with the plaster flaking off the scribbled walls, and only a knocked-up table and a few forms as furniture besides a shelf or two made by the last regiment, the whole lit by one candle and the fire of a brazier, can seem positively homely.

Lumley and I came on ahead here from the other ruins to do the billeting, which was quite a simple affair this time. The C.O. says we bagged the best billets for our two respective Companies, but I don't know. Anyway his orders are that we change over next time we're here. There is room for two colonies of officers in this building—the roof of which is intact, so that we of A and Sankey and his subordinates live, with a door between us, without interfering with one another. Our beds are sacking stretched on wooden frames, and a Wolsey valise on the top of this makes you really comfortable. The *Sketch* pictures were transported from the last billet, and no time was lost in sticking them up here. We have two bedrooms, a mess-room and a kitchen. My platoon lives in a suite of really snug apartments across the way.

At present we have a regiment of one of the new formations attached to us for instruction, as we were to the Connaughts in the summer. They come from a part of the world where the dialect is very pronounced "look you." One platoon is attached to this Company; also their officer, who is I suppose typically Kitchener, the accent only faintly noticeable.

The post was most exciting to-day. Very many thanks. The mince-pies will appear to-night, the plum pudding I shall send to the depôt (along with Hewlett's port) and then I can get it at the psychological moment.

Dear Mother, it must have been a blow to hear of our move, but it is nothing like as bad as it sounds. You see the periods are short now-a-days. Besides—*Nativitatis tempore (censoris causa per obscura dico) haud in fossis erimus, at oppidulo in quodam requiescentes.* Get Father to translate that.

I took the working party to-day ; being lucky in having my turn come in the morning and not at night. It was a cushy job behind the firing line. The war raged around and in front of us—behind were our field-guns popping off gaily, the burst of their shrapnel showing white against that famous wood behind the enemy's line ; now and then we heard a German shell whizzing towards our front line—while we worked placidly on.

My British Warm with its new collar is a perfect boon. I wear my trenchcoat up there, and as soon as we come out, on goes the other, and I can look comparatively unlike the working classes again. And I haven't yet tired of the pleasure of having fur round my neck.

I have just had a letter from Mrs. Holliday, who promises a cake. It is so kind of her and she writes at length.

Strange as it may sound my mind has never been so much at rest as when we are in the trenches—Cambridge was a turmoil in comparison.

Your Red Cross efforts are superb.

JACK

18th December 1915

DEAR MOTHER AND ALL

Here I sit in the failing light amid a muddy desolation, and, obeying warnings about the post, send now a Christmas greeting from the trenches. I am sitting with my back to the parapet; before me are the trees of a ruined orchard; dimly seen beyond are the walls of a few wrecked houses, and out of sight behind a sandbag buttress stands what is left of *——. It sounds gloomy I daresay, but "the mind is its own place" &c. Incidentally the weather is mild and no rain has fallen all this misty day—so misty that snipers have had hardly a target and the guns less—and we can carry life on as placidly as the heart could wish. And to-morrow evening—civilization again.

But while we shall be making the best of a bad job, and making it very well and merrily, for you I am afraid Christmas will be sad. That is the fly in our ointment. May it be as happy and hopeful as possible. I can only wish for you my own peace of mind.

I have seen lately officers of Billy's regiment. Two went up the road past our late billet and I caught them up, and another came along the trenches this morning. They all confirm what I had heard: that

*Neuve Chapelle.

Billy was one of the very few that reached the enemy wire. His company was ahead and he led out the front platoon, and raced across. He was last seen kneeling in front of the German wire firing his revolver, and carrying on with it after he had been hit.

For us life has gone very calmly. Christmas parcels arrive for the officers, and we live in increasing luxury. Could I have some cigars? I found one of my men smoking one this morning in his dug-out, and the whiff of it was enticing. Socks occasionally are acceptable.

With best love and wishes to all.

JACK

20th December 1915

DEAR MOTHER

Here we are in *———, with the mud scraped off (woe to those who haven't done so) and parcels continually arriving that promise tables groaning with costly piles. Duties too are light and it seems to be a real rest.

Yesterday of course in the trenches—sitting here I can hardly believe we were in that desolation such a short time ago—there was a perfect orgy of handing over to representatives of the incoming regiments. Then by the early moonlight we moved out; the reserve line was thronged with unfamiliar officers and stranded Tommies, and it was obvious there had been misunderstandings and confusions. There was a comic atmosphere of fuming and indignation, of which

* Vieille Chapelle

Hewlett had had the full benefit. Controversy had raged round him as to what dug-outs belonged exactly to which regiment, and really it was rather muddling. We, however, trekked away, leaving others to carry on the war, while the shaking flares fell further and further, and the rifles and machine guns cracked and hammered fainter. Always returning to billets one gets the feeling that the war is somehow a hallucination, so re-assuring are the cottages with cosy lit windows and roofs intact. We reached the village at last and got the men into their billets. In a few minutes they were all wearing the fur coats that awaited them and became suddenly a herd of sheep dogs, a few indeed peers of the realm. Our own billet seems superb, though the room was practically bare ; but I found the familiar in a far cheerier room with white panelled walls that looked wonderful by contrast with our late surroundings. Our supper was a cheerful affair, and we went to real beds with the prospect of a late reveille.

Only the mildest activities the next morning, and then Hewlett told me his horse would be ready immediately after lunch to ride into †—— to get money for men going on pass. The horse in question is a beauty, about the only good one in the regiment, with an exquisite action which is like sailing to the rider, and after a first furious career—unintended by me—down the village street, scattering the soldiery like chickens, I proceeded with more dignity and the greatest pleasure. Sensational reports reached headquarters of my wild charge towards the trenches; it was whispered that I was last seen with the horse caught up in the German wire.

† Merville

But here I must stop for the post tho' there is heaps to say.

JACK

Countless parcels rapturously received.

22nd December 1915

DEAR MOTHER

My last letter broke off suddenly. I was telling you about our departure from the trenches and subsequent adventures. The afternoon we came out there was a strafe by the German gunners opposite, nothing really, but more than we remembered to have had. It was all the C.O.'s fault, as he had asked our gunners to fire at a certain spot; the result was immediate retaliation of unlooked-for violence. Winser, as it happened, was on his way round the trenches when it began, and we stood together under the lee of the parapet and watched the fun, the C.O. anxiously wondering when he could get back to H.Q. Presently it was all over and everyone picked up the thread, and life proceeded normally.

We made an effective entrance into *———the next day, I on Hewlett's dainty Tango, trotting exquisitely; Hammill, on the same errand, jogging in on his fat chestnut, and Sankey behind on a black horse that would hardly move, the whole attended by a troop of little boys proffering their services as horse holders.

I returned to a cheerful tea and a host of parcels and important news. There had been a grand shuffle of officers. The job I was getting a few weeks ago has

*Merville.

definitely gone to another, a personable and very nice young man from the Bodleian Library (where he worked apparently at cataloguing books) with a cultured accent and manner. Johnson has left us, to our sorrow, for his original C, and among other changes, I, in Hammill's absence, take over command and pay of B Company. So here I am, by an alien but very friendly hearth. Lumley has gone to command C, but didn't want to leave B's very comfortable billet, so he is with us at meals ; an excellent arrangement socially, and most useful to me. Then there is the R. C. Padre (attached to us) whom I didn't care for when I first met him a few weeks back, but he turns out to be the most capital and convivial creature, full of wisdom and charity of heart. Next comes ———, a mere boy and rather spoilt, but otherwise all right. Last comes the astonishing ———. He is about thirty-six, and has spent the greater part of his life among Esquimaux and such in Northernest Canada; the result is a sort of wild appearance, as of a raven, tho' his enormous eyes are rather attractively expressive. He gives the impression of a kindly hawk. Peace as an end and consummation of our warfarings means nothing beautiful or even interesting to him ; comfort, fireside, meals, &c., have no appeal. Even now he is longing to get back to the trenches, where he would prefer to stay all the time and be a sort of trench bailiff (much as Lycidas was guardian of the shore). He was continually out on patrol when we were there and is a dissentient voice in most of our councils. He is also the most casual person in the world, and has a dreamy manner and a rather soft intonation. He is almost unquestionably a bit mad, but full of useful suggestion and sound judgment I think.

Again I must stop. You can imagine I am busy just now.

The Fortnum and Mason things are splendid, and we shall have a regal feast. Margaret's hand-warmers I have found invaluable. The other things I will duly acknowledge.

JACK

B. E. F., FRANCE
3rd January 1916

DEAR MOTHER

At last!

Hammill is back, and I feel like a swimmer in smooth water again. I am staying on with B who are short of officers at present. Also we are out of the trenches just now and going further back on the morrow, so it is roses all the way!

Considering how small a command a company is, comparatively, it is extraordinary how many things crop up to harass the mind; it would have been a simple affair in my native A.

It is so long since I described anything in detail that I must start with how we spent Christmas Day.

After breakfast I went up to the Company Office to arrange for the distribution of the many and various gifts supplied by newspapers and other well-wishers. I was just settling down when a message came along summoning all Company Commanders, mounted, to the Brigade Office. Off I went for the Company horse, leaving the distribution of largess to another. We foregathered at the gates before the smiling Sewell, (who is now confirmed as Staff-Captain), Hewlett on his neat mount, self, Lumley in new trench coat, and Sankey. The rise of the road to bridge a canal a bit further along reminded me strongly of English roads crossing our railway lines. It was soft weather, with a suggestion of sunlight dimmed by possible rain. Winser was of the party and did polo stunts with Hewlett as we rode away. Our errand was to have a look at the billets we were to take over on our way to the firing line in a day or two. Through the long winding street of half-deserted —— we went, with gunners and drivers straightening deferentially. The road was full of shell-holes. We reached the spot—which we had inhabited before on our way to the Glory Hole—and guides took each of us to the Company billets. I found the officers that concerned me living in a state indescribable. At a table sat the Company Commander, a young Captain who was at Camberley, strongly reminiscent of Bunny Burton, without his charm. (I am told he is a journalist.) On the floor were the valises of his subalterns, and over these (the valises) stepped the servants, about their occasions, towards another table littered with food and garbage. The journalist seemed perfectly content, though had they stirred a finger they could have found themselves self-respecting billets. I made a resolve that this should not be when I took over, and went the round. Then got my horse again and rode away. Was it really Christmas? Behind were occasional crashes of heavy German shells, and I heard a machine gun of ours hammer. On my return I found that Harvey had got practically all the presents (shaving mirrors, pocket writing cases, pipes, tobacco, sweets, &c.) off his hands. The next job was to arrange the mid-day "binge." The Sergeant-Major had rigged up one of the barns with tables and plank seats ; some R.E. material had obviously been filched from somewhere, but I think we gave it all back. The plum-puddings to which you subscribed had not come, but we gave them roast instead of stew—there were some quite good potatoes, some real stout secured in —— by Jones, and Harvey bought a lot of oranges. It was a terrific job getting the men all in and the meat served round (by the N.C.O.'s), just like a school treat, but it was managed somehow. Winser came round and was vociferously cheered. As he was leaving a man turned up who had already refreshed himself elsewhere, and treated the C.O. very solemnly to a sort of chant with bell-ringing obligato, swinging his hands, very realistically, as if he had the instruments there and was in front of a leisured family in England. The Sergeants were by this time due for the Sergeants' " binge " at H.Q., a magnificent affair, and I managed to get a table for the Corporals, who were not included but had served the men, in the Company office, and they had a comfortable feed there. Then we retired.

I had ordered a large consignment of rolls for the men's tea, but Harvey had bought them so much bread that I was very glad to take them instead to A Company as an offering. Luckily they hadn't started tea, so Hewlett got the platoon sergeants up each with a sack, and we distributed the rolls according to the numbers required. I had tea with Hewlett and Mellenfield, which seemed quite like home.

By this time an invitation had come from H.Q. to the officers of B Company and the R.C. Padre. At first we were bored, having planned out our own feast, with all the various foods from our homes, and Sankey and Garvin as honoured guests, to share Mrs. Winser's champagne and your cherry brandy. But that was put off to the next night, and up we went greatly wondering why on us had fallen this honour, for no others were invited.

You may picture us then at H.Q. in a well-lighted comfortable room with a large mantlepiece and open fireplace; over the table hung a chandelier with candles burning. The table had a clean white cloth, and was loaded with all the time-honoured sweets in lavish display. Winser at one end of the table looked superb, and produced quite a homely and fatherlike effect. At the other end was ——, pale and witty, with his extraordinary appearance, which to sympathisers becomes a distinction. On his left was the Doctor—*locum tenens* for our M.O., who was getting married in England—quite a personality, a young man who has knocked about in remote Balkan holes and corners; he has a pale and sallow complexion and the most level-headed expression you could wish for; the cool and confident poise of his head is a study for a sculptor; then came Lumley, smiling and epigrammatic and smart; next him old Harper, the Quarter-Master; at the end the C.O.; on his left the Padre, fat-faced and kindly; then Harvey, who displayed an unsuspected genius for uncorking bottles; myself; Anderson (B Company's latest), efficient and coming refreshingly from the North of England; on his left Vellacott. It was a happy affair; we drank, you may be sure, to absent friends. Sewell was rung up and made to come along; he turned up and reported a certain dullness at Brigade H.Q., but only stayed a few minutes. A bowl of punch was brought in and cards suggested. I said I would teach them Newmarket, though I couldn't remember the rules. That game was the most refreshing thing I have had for some time; nobody else knew the rules, but they gradually returned to me. Before we settled down everybody ragged and seized the prizes on any pretext; amusement was also caused by the joker, which Vellacott and Lumley contrived to smuggle back into the pack every hand, and it invariably turned up among the Padre's cards. Then we settled down and had a first-class round. It seemed then to be really Christmas; all cares were forgotten.

The next day we were inspected, a Company at a time, by the new Divisional General. There was a wind, and I nearly strained my vocal chords shouting down the line. As he turned away I heard him say to Winser: "A good Company."

The next day we moved to the new billets, the Padre accompanying. Life there was fairly uneventful, though for me crowded.

It would be against all the rules to describe our last time in the trenches, dearly as I should like to do so. From the nature of the case it was most weird and amusing; also for me most worrying, and I grew very irritable at times. For one thing I had very little support. We had an officer attached for instruction, of whom of course little could be expected; Anderson I had not with me. ——— is one of the best fellows in the world, and splendid with the men, but for certain parts of an officer's job in the trenches intentionally useless. He is a wild creature, with no love of forms and rules and times; living as he has done for years on his own among Indians and Esquimaux and the like, his interest in things is spasmodic. But he was killingly funny at times. After hours of lethargy and apathy I would hear him by night, in the pauses of the wind, cursing and strafing at sentries who hadn't loaded, in a croaky voice audible in the German lines probably. The next moment he might have vaulted over the parapet with his revolver without warning anyone. He is the chief patrolling officer in the Regiment, quite a patrol fiend. He found out innumerable details about the ground between the lines, and would never tell me so that I could report it. I shan't easily forget him the first morning we were there. The light grew and revealed the details of the land, and —— stood there regardless of possible snipers, shouting out discoveries as the strengthening light brought them, roaring comments and conjectures to the general air—keenness personified like a dog on a trail. Also he threw a bomb into our wire, calling the world to witness. Our attached officer, with his plaintive gentle voice, was a foil to him. A Company relieved us last night, and I gathered my flock together and out we came. Hammill was waiting for us at the reserve billets, and I must say it was soothing to hand over to him.

We are living in a deserted house of a prosperous class; bare walls but great comfort. There is actually an open fireplace here. Old Hammill is a perfect dear.

This morning —— and I had to go to H.Q. and report on the ground we left last night. I expected a strafing, but it was very pleasant. It was a perfect morning, clear as the Spring. As we went along the road a hare was sighted half-right in a field. Instantly —— with a shout was across the ditch-land stalking, revolver in hand. We had a desperate discussion over sketches and maps as to the precise lie of ditches. I thought we should never get through. I managed to evolve some sort of a report at last. ——, especially to a Company Commander, can be the most trying and exasperating creature in the world, but everybody loves him. He does things with a zest and a keenness of expression that recall Bliss (from whom I had a letter this evening); he has the kindest heart and a fund of humour.

To-morrow we return to the sheltering wing of the Padre.

It is such a pleasure to be able to write to you again. Meanwhile parcels have arrived innumerable and have remained unacknowledged—sweets, cakes and what not.

Enough for the nonce.

JACK.

5th January 1916

DEAR MOTHER

Here we are in ———* again. Stacks of room for everybody, as the late occupants were as the sand on the sea shore, and occupied hosts of billets we had otherwise left untouched. I am still with B but may return to A any moment. Winser, who likes

*Merville.

his little joke—indeed Headquarters are notorious legpullers, as I told Vellacott to his surprise and consternation—said last night that I should be going to D to-morrow. This I can hardly credit.

Will you tell Father that the gloves are the glove perfect at last. I would write to him but there is not time for both. Margaret sent me a number of happily chosen Stevensons—which I received with delight.

I had an amusing day yesterday. I was detailed to do the billetting for the Battalion, and arriving early in the morning at the Brigade Office for instructions from Sewell, found Hewlett's groom and the dainty Tango waiting. It was quite a long ride through more and more peaceful and prosperous a countryside, till the big elaborate tower of Charpentier's ambitious church loomed nearer. Passing a billet I was hailed by name and out ran Ellis, once a master at the Rileys and one of the best of fellows. He spoke sympathetically about Geoffrey.

It was a pleasure to enter a town again, and see the clustered haunts of men, second rate and rather shoddy as this place is.

The people in occupation were a newer battalion of Billy's regiment. The company who had our A's billets gave me lunch. The Second in Command—whose chief was not present—was a pleasant voluptuary; they did themselves proud. It was amusing to come to our old billets; Madame was in raptures and hailed the prospect of greeting Hewlett again. The regiment gave me rather a good impression; they had a certain vigour; various improvements and innovations were afoot and officers and men kept themselves very spruce.

I was wearing my trench uniform and contrasted with them. I should be much interested to see them again after a few weeks of the mud and sand-bags. As it was they gave an impression of freshness; of gallant adventurers at the threshold of experience ; Brigade and Divisional instructions which I saw gave evidence of people nerved up for enterprise, with an ardour for detail much of which will doubtless soon be forgotten, trodden in the trench-mud. Sitting there I felt strangely experienced.

When they had gone—the officers were going up to have a preliminary nose round—I started on a grand tour of the billeting area, which was slightly altered from last time and needed a little thought in adjusting. It was an interesting round, and an officer I met in one of the company billets was a model of courtesy. Having arranged the company areas, I went back to our place and made a plan, and then collected Hewlett's groom and returned through the falling dusk. The Regiment was just entering their new billets a little further back when I got in. It was the place we left for the trenches. There was the Padre, having collected masses of food; it was a jolly foregathering in the Company Headquarters with Hammill back and the return to *———— in prospect for the morrow. Life seemed all rosy. It was misty as we went down the road to our sleeping place. Across the fields, not so far away, the lights rose and quivered; at a distance they are like balls of lit thistledown, so softly and airily do they spring and fall. Now and then the lower rims of the cloud-bank flickered, lit by an unheard Battery's flashes. What

*Merville

did it all matter?—we were leaving it. As one leaves the trenches and looks back, the sight of that nightly game renewed is an unceasing wonder.

The morning broke with soft airs and sun-light, perfect weather for the opening of a year. The troops came along very well. Our entry into —— was triumphant with shouts and singing.

That was yesterday. To-day the C.O. inspected us; we expected appalling strafings on the discovery of our various omissions; but at the outset it was obvious that the whole thing was going to go off like a harlequinade, the which it did. The C.O. looked superb, a Hermes, if a little sterner in outline. To-morrow is to be a rest-day I believe.

I will tell you about the men later.

JACK

13th January 1916

DEAR FATHER

It was long ago that you asked various questions. My period in command of this Company intervened and drove most things out of my head.

"Hopeless Dawn" (which was the title of a picture in the Academy some years back, if I remember aright) we apply to those early mornings when the prospect is rather grim. A case in point was our waking up one morning in ——*, when we had slept

*Festubert

in a dusty corner of barely rain-proof ruins, and woke to a cold sleety world with muddy trenches in prospect. We said the same of the following morning, when Hewlett and I woke rather cold in an unattractive dug-out, with mud all round.

The "trough" was a word I applied to the officers' mess in a front line we held. You see the inside of the dug-out was roughly like the inside of a tram; you sat at one seat, as it were, with your feet in the central passage and ate off the other seat, which was the only table available. It was merely as if the mud floor of the place had a trough dug down the middle to accommodate the feet of occupants.

The date of my second star was the 17th April. It wasn't in the Gazette till well on in May. The captain you spoke of wasn't appointed to this regiment.

May I have some more cigarettes? The cigars are excellent and much admired by my friends. The cycling cape was a godsend, and the gloves just the thing.

JACK.

The Dispatch Rider book is obviously first-rate.

13th January 1916

DEAR MOTHER
Many thanks for your long letter.

I have just come from a typical native discussion. Enter a lonely figure, in the light blue French uniform (I confess to complete ignorance of our allies' uniforms;

this may have been an officer or a sergeant). He addresses himself to Hammill who is making notes for a lecture, and anyway can't speak French; so the intruder is "passed to" me "for necessary action, please". Evidently the affair is some claim for damages;. it transpires that somebody in the last regiment took away part of a bicycle lamp that was hanging in the bedroom. One of the boys, a nice fellow, shows me where it hung. By this time the whole family has poured in, to the consternation of Hammill, and everyone is talking. I order an adjournment to the next room, where our servants sit round with wondering eyes among the preparations for to-night's dinner. As far as I remember we all talked during the actual move, the family walking backwards and gesticulating. Any way the door was left open. By this time Madame was taking an ell; like a Macbeth witch she laid on my arm a distinctly choppy finger. It appeared that there had also been some scandalous affair connected with a mouth organ; the mess room too had not been paid for; the last officer had apparently behaved very much amiss. It was quite understood, and everybody repeated it in turn with emphasis, that it wasn't us but the last occupants who had done these things; but Madame was probably using my sympathetic ear as a receptacle for her grievances. The whole thing subsided as rapidly as it had begun, by a final and concerted repetition that the last occupants and certainly not we were to blame, and the French official departed among perfectly cordial farewells.

Hammill and I went and looked at the church yesterday. There is some fine wood-work round the sides; otherwise the decoration is as cheap and gaudy as the framework of a merry-go-round, though always impressive and pleasing I think from the west end of the building.

I had a letter yesterday from Gilbert, who finds that the lingering effects of the sunstroke that he had in India will prevent him going with his companions of the Ambulance to Egypt, but he will try to get a job in this country. I told him to go over to Bakewell, but he only gets leave very rarely, and that short.

Can I have another of these writing pads?

JACK

16th January 1916

DEAR MOTHER
I think you will need to have no anxiety about us for some time now, according to what they tell us.

We are settling down in this uneventful village to systematic training; and the war seems a far cry. I haven't heard a gun for days. But I suppose at this minute, back there, patrols are crawling across the desolate grass, wading the flooded ditches with caution lest the water splash, and sentries stare out to see what they can see, which is very little, as an enemy flare lights for a moment the quaint stakes that hold the wire. And we sit here, with the tea things clustered round the lamp.

On Saturday the C.O. inspected us all together. A battalion parade is almost always comic, as nearly everyone is slightly on edge, and this was no exception. Our C.O. and Adjutant of course make an amusing contrast to watch, Vellacott looking the personification of insolent scorn (until you catch his eye). Praise and blame were freely scattered. There was hardly room for a battalion in the field chosen, and when the standing part was finished and we moved about, the ground became more and more trodden and muddy. Movements were necessarily limited, and involved circling round and round the space at our disposal until we looked like the snake that ate its tail.

I now consider myself completely conversant with the latest pattern bomb. The C.O. hauled some of us out on Saturday afternoon to the bombing ground we've made; and we threw the things, dummy and live, and took them to pieces. Most of us sat behind a haystack while one threw.

Sunday began calmly, but pressure developed later, as we had to hustle off part of the troops to get baths some miles off. I walked along the canal to ——* to get cash for the men. It was a longish but very pleasant expedition. As I came back it was as hard as ever to realize the war. The straight procession of tall trees that marked the tow-path stood without the motion of a twig, as if they guarded the Sleeping Beauty's Palace; not a ripple down the stretching water, and no suggestion of life in the dark heavy barges; the moon was somewhere behind a thin veil of cloud and it was strangely light. The illusion was broken presently by

*Merville.

the rattling and lumbering of a limbered waggon, and one of our transport drivers, with a Canadian accent, hailing the people of an estaminet in good French.

Hammill and I were staggered last night by the arrival from H.Q. of our programme of work for the week, detailing the number of hours to be spent on the various subjects. We had to get to and make out our scheme. It worked quite well to-day.

Cigarettes for the troops (Wills's abominable "Woodbine") would be acceptable. The Padre (R.C.) is running a recreation room where a few things are sold and would welcome contributions. He is a most excellent man, tinderest teacher, and koindliest crature, and appears to have won the heart of the C.O., who attended his service yesterday.

I am so glad Margaret is going to the Burkitts'. Give Philip Abraham my love if he is still about when this comes. Here too on hedge and tree are a myriad little brown buds. Teddy, writing some time back, said that in the Spring surely we should see daylight. I think Spring must always bring hope.

JACK

23rd January 1916

DEAR MOTHER

Very many thanks for the mittens. Hammill is much pleased.

As I said we have an incredible programme for next week. It starts with a Brigade route march to-morrow morning. Attacks on the village are to be made later with bombs and machine guns. We have a certain amount of social life after the labours of the day. B Company had a concert the other night. It was quite like old days to hear the audience applaud the sighs of jilted swains and long-drawn out tragedies of domestic life. Vellacott dined with us the other night; we propounded a scheme of shortening or at least enlivening the war by arranging a charge of elephants on the German trenches. Last night C Company gave a concert, and Hammill, the Padre and I went as Lumley's guests. There were more domestic tragedies and lovers' yearnings (which were more successful than the comic turns). The part we enjoyed was a great effort by the sergeants; the Sergeant-Major lifted the back curtain of the tent and they trooped in in costume, having apparently rifled the villagers; there were peasants, male and female, a piou-piou and the conductor with bâton and German accent complete. They looked killing, but didn't let themselves go half enough. Afterwards we all went on to supper at Lumley's and made merry over sandwiches and stout. It seemed the last word in luxury behind the line.

Yesterday we sent working parties to make a rifle range near the forest. This involved crossing the canal, a considerable undertaking. We arrived at an estaminet which seemed to be the starting place of the *barque*. A high wind was blowing and the stout old lady I interviewed regarded the enterprise with distaste. She began however to manipulate a punt pole, and was presently joined by the daughter, a stalwart and very capable if faintly sinister damsel, who promptly took command and ferried a hundred men in numerous drafts in masterful fashion. She treated the soldiery with complete indifference if not contempt, and had an odd way of glancing sideways at nothing, which was rather roguish.

We were building the stop-butts of a range, a much more pukka affair than the other I wrote of, and we looked like a host of Egyptians building a pyramid. At one point there was a race between B and A's party, with brilliant results; it was like a beehive; I never saw so much work done in a few minutes. We returned by a different ferry; at the first the man refused to take us, apparently not liking his craft to be used for military operations. We went on to the next and interviewed an enthusiastic and plaintive woman; she too was stout, but made some overtures with the pole; then a much stouter, and in fact quite shapeless, companion wrested the pole from her and was on the point of bringing the boat across to us, when our previous acquaintance, the man, darted up and leapt aboard. The first woman watched the embarcation of the whole force in some trepidation; she was all against having more than six at a time. There was, however, no hitch. Sitting there waiting our turn, Jones and I thought it would seem quite natural to see eight long yellow oars flash round the bend of the reach; Jones was at Oxford.

Everything has looked lovely to-day; it has been clear and sunny and a thought colder, less mild that is. If it carries on like this the horrors of a winter campaign on this front are negligible.

The new Brigadier is most active, knocking about all the time.

The second of those football bladders I took out came in very usefully for the company this afternoon; can I have one or two more? The Christmas plum-puddings did come, a day late. We got some more from the *Daily News* yesterday; they were much enjoyed to-day. Various gifts come for the troops; mouth organs trickle in, and the other day there was chocolate from various colonies, in very decorative boxes.

JACK

26th January 1916

DEAR MOTHER

Isn't the weather wonderful? It seems almost Spring already.

I have just come back from escorting a party to the baths. They get these in the ground floors of mills and other such establishments, sitting in tubs amid clouds of steam, like figures in an Inferno. They are given a complete change of underclothing.

Meanwhile we carry on, tho' our programmes, flourishing in weekly with so much ado, don't materialise so menacingly as they promise. The background of our parades is the canal with its row of tall thin trees, all slightly bent one way and without a branch till they feather out at the top. Transport and Red-Cross motors pass continually up and down the broad tow-path, and, beyond, trains of great barges or a tug with a hospital barge. In the evening it is the "wide-winged sunset of the misty marsh." On clear days sometimes when they are firing we hear the guns, faint short rumblings.

Harvey, one of our officers, I am getting to like very well. He is one of the Canadian products. He astonished me yesterday by two drawings, one labelled "Rest," the other "Grief;" subjects set I believe by the Padre. The latter is going to set another and Harvey and I will have a competition, tho' I fear I can't compete with his skill. I am reading Dickens' Hard Times, a copy of Hammill's that we raked up out of the Company's stores.

Excuse a dull letter.

JACK

27th January 1916

DEAR MOTHER

I was simply delighted to hear of your pleasant day, and to hear from Father that Kitty had got leave at the auspicious moment. I received this afternoon a pleasing selection of sweets —— the ginger especially —— and the many socks and mittens have come. The socks we are keeping till the trenches.

Here in this secluded hamlet we pursue our even course far from the noise of the archers.

This morning each Company was inspected in turn by the new Brigadier. We had to give the troops some coaching to pronounce his name, and their efforts to do so helped to pass away the longish time he kept us waiting for his arrival. In appearance he is mild, suggesting an elderly eagle, and he has an odd way of standing with slightly open mouth and a bland expression, his head shaking. I am sorry to say I was ticked off by the C.O. (who looked superb) for my equipment, which tho' clean is in bad repair and hangs but ill. For the rest of the time I was hovering round in a vague manner, as a Company Second in Command didn't seem to be recognised ; there was an awful squash in between the ranks of each platoon, when, having finished with the back views of the front rank, we turned to see the front aspect of the rear one ; there was the General, the Platoon Commander (anxious), the C.O., Hammill, self, the Company Sergeant-Major, the Company Quarter-Master Sergeant, and the Battalion S.M.. the last three with faces like boots, as Margaret says ; the Brigade Major was fortunately off inspecting rifles. This unique procession invariably jammed at the flank of each platoon. His scrutiny with its accompaniment of questions reminiscent of Sir Joseph Porter, K.C.B. over, the General required that Harvey should make the company do an evolution or two. As I was doubtful whether Harvey knew the word of command I suggested to Hammill that I should perform ; Hammill thought that this was not the G.O.C.'s intention, and we had time to whisper formulas to Harvey while the General was taking some notes. Harvey then carried on, and was vastly disturbed and put out for the rest of the day on observing the latter turn and take more notes. Anderson was then called out (I being passed over unnoticed) and did a stunt or two. ———— recently returned from Div. H.Q., we had carefully kept off parade as an erratic and discordant element. The Brigadier then thanked Hammill, saying the company was quite satisfactory ; the Brigadier declared the rifles to be good, and the gilded circle withdrew to fresh hunting grounds.

————, as I said, is back dissatisfied, as I suppose he will be with any job he gets in the army. You see having lived so long on his own, and becoming "closely assimilated to the Indians in his manner of life" he can't bear being tied down or given orders. Shortly after his return he disappeared to the neighbouring town for his kit, and came back carrying a stove in which were his worldly goods. It wasn't the first we had heard of that stove, for which he had searched all available French towns. He has brought a dog too called Miquin ; a sort of young collie.

I have heard from Wadsworth, who is billeted at Army Head Quarters; whither too the Padre departed to-day in search, as he says, of a gramophone, the second time he has gone to the same place on that errand. I have had also a charming letter from old Essen, who says he will meet me at any hour of the day or night anywhere to grasp my hand, if ever I come to England; that however is not to be for some time.

How beautiful about Geoffrey's letter.* Will you send it to the Neuffers after the war ? I like to think of the last time we met, that merry party in Plymouth, and how much we all enjoyed each others society, he and Vaudrey and I.

JACK

29th January 1916

DEAR MOTHER
I received a copy to-day of a very jolly and characteristic letter of Teddy's, written while wandering apparently among the scattered vestiges of old civilizations.

*Ten days before war broke out Geoffrey terminated a stay of seven happy months with a German family. Among his papers was found, written on his return home, a letter thanking his hostess, Frau Neuffer, for her many kindnesses. The letter did not get through to Germany but was returned to the writer.

We meander placidly on. All the officers went up to H.Q. two nights ago for a lecture. It transpired that Hewlett was billed to appear, but he didn't turn up, and the C.O. therefore carried on about other subjects. In the middle, the door opened and there entered a native, a smiling youth of excellent complexion, who wanted to explain something about somebody else who was now brought in, the very opposite of himself, a pale and weedy person with untidy black hair. The C.O. is not a linguist, and Lumley's invaluable services were called for. It was quite an odd scene; round the room sat the assembled subalterns, by the door was Lumley, in excellent French elucidating the difficulties of the pale and refugee-like individual; the other youth seemed to enjoy the proceedings mightily, and the C.O. towered over the group with interjections in English.

The next morning most of us left the troops to the care of N.C.O.'s, and had a sort of pedestrian staff ride, the subject being the attack and defence of the village. Garvin and Lumley, with their respective subordinates, defended the place from our theoretic attack. We moved about the buildings in dubious groups while the C.O. went from one to another with advice. We found eventually that Lumley's defensive dispositions were far different from what we had expected; there followed long arguments, in the course of which one or two of us went up the church tower ostensibly to inpect the range of Lumley's ten picked shots. The main upshot was that we have all to write out a description of what we would do, which is tiresome.

In the evening the Divisional Follies were billed to appear in ——*, and I went, as I had met on another occasion the R.F.A. subaltern who does actor-manager (I had sat in the green-room while the company made themselves up). It was quite a refreshing affair with an atmosphere of stageland ; they do the pierrot touch, but are not half ambitious enough I think, considering the time and opportunity at their disposal ; the gunner is one of those very suave people—deuced good fellows don't yer know—who are really quite fun, and scattered at wide enough intervals to make them very agreeable companions when met with. On the last occasion we wrung each other's hands at parting ; this time of course he was rather pre-occupied.

Yesterday we went and fired on the range we had sent working parties to the week before, as described in a previous despatch. It was now quite a smart affair. It was just that Saturday, the last in January, that we finished our firing a twelve-month ago at Perham Down, on an unforgettable afternoon when the light lingered, and the plain was a glorious harmony of blues and greens and yellows; but now it was a dead-still foggy afternoon, and in the firing, without a pause, a muffled thumping of guns.

Terry, the doctor, came to dinner. He is a simply charming man, who took the job over last November, and is now going, to all our regrets. We talked long, the conversation taking the form of Padre *contra mundum*.

To-morrow we move still further back. Am I to return the copy of Teddy's letter ?

JACK.

*Merville

31st January 1916

Dear Mother

Here we are, after, for us, quite an adventurous day. We are further back than we have ever been since July. We started out quite early this morning and trekked away through familar scenes where we had our first impressions of France. It all looked very different of course with the bare trees. But we feel that winter is almost over.

At last we experienced what we haven't had for ages, a real hill; none of us had moved up a slope for many a day; it felt quite like home. The men were all talking about the " broo." The halt for the midday meal was most picturesque. I tried to draw it for you but couldn't get the right atmosphere. We had reached country very like Salisbury Plain and the Wiltshire Downs; the spot might well have been somewhere near Andover, with its restful outlines. The regiment sat on the side of the road that swept in a broad curve along the downs; below was the shallow open valley with woods and mist. The field cookers, smoking vigorously, came rolling up amid resounding cheers and everybody was happy; the existence of the last fortnight suddenly seemed quite stuffy. When we proceeded, the country was still varied and interesting; there was one steepish wooded slope that recalled the Wye valley down to Haddon. We climbed one hill that was really puffing and emerged on top with the world like a map at our feet. White roads meandered through the country displayed below. About three o'clock we reached this village, and set about getting fixed in. The barn Lumley had allotted to two of our platoons was only half big enough, and I had to trot round looking for further accommodation. The country we had passed through was nothing like so dotted with small holdings as the district we had inhabited before, and all up the rising village street are thick wall like fortifications or prison-walls, and looking through the arched entrances you saw stately farms of considerable size, all very dignified and well established. The fact that it is not level makes it quite different from any place where we have been billeted ; and some of the buildings, have their bricks in alternate courses of red and white, the whole mellowed with age.

We are all making for early bed. To-morrow I hear we practise the attack, Clevedon fashion.

JACK

2nd February 1916

DEAR MOTHER

Here we are back again, and the hills behind us. This is how it befell.

Yesterday morning found us all preparing for the attack, a day of roaming over the downs amid the exhortations or curses of Commanders on prancing horses. Just before parade a message came along to the effect that we weren't to use the ground in question, that the day would be a holiday and that we should return to our former billets on the morrow. It brought us sorrow mixed with joy; the prospect of this place again was rather dull. But a holiday was delightful. In a moment the troops were wandering about in leisurely groups. We inspected their feet and a disquisition was made to the N.C.O.'s. After which the Padre Harvey and I started off in holiday mood for a jaunt to the neighbouring town*, which I had long wanted to see. It was a day full of early spring, the veiled sun turned the mist to pale colours like a pearl, and, lighting on the warm brown walls of some farm-buildings, set them in relief against the fields where the light did not strike, and which were just a haze of vague tints. As we went along it seemed that we had snatched a day out of the past by some artifice; the war was for the moment a freak of fancy, though the guns still rumbled away eastward, as indeed they had hardly left off doing for days. We were extremely delighted when we reached the farm-buildings aforesaid. Opposite the house the garden wall gave way to railings, as if the architect had wished that passers-by should have the chance of enjoying his work. And certainly we enjoyed it; we had stood there for a minute or two when the sun came through the light clouds and sent the shadows of the trees across the lawn. The south face of the house opened with French windows on the garden and looked as if it had mellowed in the warmth of many summers.

It was extraordinary to think of the people who lived in this stately place, within sound of the war, a short motor ride from the mud and the rat-haunted dug-outs. The next delight was a spring by the road that welled up very clean and abundant in a graceful basin of brick. Shortly afterwards we reached the outskirts of ———*. An ugly new villa with all the

*Aire.

formulas, including ornamental water and pea-cocks (rather dowdy), provoked a discussion whether religion has a good effect on domestic architectute, as the Padre declared that only atheists could inhabit such a house. At the side we approached from, at any rate, the town had none of the usual defects of a town's edge. Quite suddenly we had reached a square, beyond which the street that led to the centre of the town was most picturesque with its quaint roofs and gables. When we reached the Grand Place it seemed we were in another world. It was as if a magician had taken the great court of Trinity and made alterations suitable for the main square of a town; though this was much larger of course. The surrounding shops and inns and houses were picturesque and harmonious, white or cream-coloured, with jolly gables; at the top of the square and fronting the whole was the Hotel de Ville, a large renaissance building of some light stone, surmounted by a beautful tower with a black clock face whose gilt figures were a joy in themselves; the gentle sunlight beat on the whole and made it seem so clean and fresh that it might have been the seat of government in an idealist's Republic. And yet there were so few people moving anywhere—the rare English officers only accentuated the loneliness—that the captured lingering sunshine in the broad silent spaces could not dispel an impression that this was a city on which an enchantment more sinister than sleep had fallen; I don't believe there was a door or window open in all those quiet houses. All the men of course had gone, some not to return. But I have never seen the like.

We passed on to the cathedral, up a quaint winding street that gave, as so often, a wonderfully effective view of the tower at its head. We spent quite a time inside, among the splendour that I suppose there always is in large R. C. churches. We lunched somewhat to our chagrin at a public table, the Padre in the middle and Harvey and I as his disciples on either hand. Afterwards we had a most spirited recital of her experiences from a woman who kept a tobacco shop in the square. I confess I only understood scraps of it until the Padre explained later. It was quite a thrilling tale, and she told it with the greatest spirit and cheerfulness. Her husband had a large business in Lille; they were separated when the Germans arrived and she lost sight of him; she applied however to the General for permission to set up the business elsewhere and Brussels was settled on. She was taken there by a German officer who treated her with every consideration. On their arrival he saw her to a hotel and arranged to meet her next morning. When he arrived with his car at the appointed hour next morning the bird was flown. She had got away by the help of some Dutch agency, intending to make for Calais. The proposed route and railway or what not proved out of the question, and they had to walk. Six days they were on the road. The way led through Louvain, where they had to cross the main square stepping over piles of bodies. By the time they reached Calais she had given up her husband; they got no papers and the enemy falsified all the news. The woman's wanderings took her to Folkestone, and back again to Calais immediately, for some reason. It was about then that in a Lille newspaper, dropped by a friendly aeroplane, she saw an advertisement from her husband applying for new premises and knew that all was comparatively well. (The Padre has come in and I find I am telling the story all wrong; it was before she was deported from Lille that the aeroplane dropped the paper which contained an advertisement from her husband in Calais, and refuted the German statements that Calais was taken; the latter then became her objective and she could only reach it by Folkestone via Holland). The couple were reunited in Calais and parted again, he to the Army, while she eventuated, as Margaret says, at ———,* where she carries on the tobacconist job in reduced circumstances.

In the evening we went round to an informal sing-song at Lumley's and I touched what I hadn't touched for months, a piano.

This morning we set out again across the hills, where a chill wind blew the dust in our faces. It was just like Salisbury Plain; we might have been crossing Beacon Hill that stretches down to Bulford. There was no notable incident to report.

It has been like some wild kind of week-end outing. I am mighty glad of it. We are all rather tired.

JACK.

3rd February 1916

DEAR MOTHER

I was so glad to hear of the silver wedding day. It was indeed luck that Kitty was home.

I was very eager to hear of Margaret's time at Cambridge. The weather here is colder, but oh! the mud is going, we really believe. We were shocked to

*Aire.

read yesterday morning that the C.O.'s father has been killed, run over in the darkened street. He has gone home for a few days.

This afternoon we attended a demonstration in the rapid construction of wire entanglements by C Company N.C.O.'s, who had been specially trained. The officers stood in a gay group and the N.C.O.'s of the regiment in discreet ranks. Bell was the impresario, and looked a very charming one. At his signal his myrmidons leapt forth, and really the thing went up like magic. Then it was taken down, and A.'s, B.'s and D.'s N.C.O.'s did it, and, to their credit, almost equally fast. By degrees the officers' comments grew more irrelevant and frivolous and the gathering broke up.

Hewlett came along later to borrow a book from me—he has now almost exhausted my library. We had a long religious discussion.

I wasn't best pleased to read of the Zeppelin raid that had visited Derbyshire. I am afraid you must be rather anxious, but I don't think much will come of it.

I had a delightful letter from Mozley, who has achieved some theological book by which he secures promotion in the ecclesiastical world. ———, home wounded, is apparently harking back to the pacificist fold, to Mozley's sorrow.

I saw in the Daily Mail, which really excels itself now, that one of its minions appears to have dined with the Kaiser at Nish, whatever that may mean—that you have been having remarkable weather in England, as here. I found in a garden of the village where we had our recent outing a cherry tree in blossom. There are numbers of leaves about.

JACK

5th February 1916
DEAR MOTHER

There was some rain after my triumphant prophecy, but it has cleared again, and the afternoon was radiant.

It is after five now, but I can still see to write at the window. The latter opens full on the road, so that our inmost lives are at the mercy of the public, and the soldiers wonder whether one salutes officers through an intervening window.

The children are entrancing. It was Hammill I think who lured them here in the first place. Now they come continually in ones and twos or in a group, and we hand them out cake and chocolates, and exchange caps. They have the jolliest clean faces. The Padre adores them. We know their names and greet them with shouts of Marcel, Andrè, and the rest. When we have had enough they scamper off with a savoir faire worthy of a count.

Father recently sent a consignment of Woodbines. They were taken to the recreation room this afternoon; the bearer came up here and returned there in a few minutes to find every one sold.

I must catch the post.

JACK

6th February 1916

DEAR MOTHER

I am quite relieved to hear that Bakewell had not been destroyed. The paper mentioned Derbyshire, and one might draw any conclusion.

Harvey and I had a jolly ride yesterday afternoon in the radiant weather, when the ploughed land looked brown and warm and the tall trees lining the canal were a picture. We passed out of the light into the forest, where everything was still and rather chilly, and roamed in and out the still trees over last year's leaves. We tried to jump the little ditches, but our horses were not enterprising. We made a triumphal return to billets at the canter, tho' the effect as far as I was concerned was spoiled by the indecent descent of my puttee.

I have really no news; we might be at Tidworth for all that happens. This morning there was an officers' revolver shooting match, at which none of us distinguished ourselves. Church Parade followed, when our Padre was no worse than usual; this afternoon I conducted a rapid wiring practice, as there is a prize-giving shortly for the quickest company team. I thought them rather slow at first, but their final performance was like lightning.

——— is with us again as the Divisional Staff don't want him at present. Indeed nobody knows quite what to do with him; he is a sort of cuckoo in the black-bird's nest. Here they have palmed "Sniping Officer" off on him, but it's not the real solution.

Our best recent acquisition is our Second in Command, a very unpretentious little man with no particular appeal at first sight; but he proves perfectly charming, with a most happy manner, no suggestion of side, and a very willing ear for what the humblest person has to say.

I look forward to our return to the trenches; they are really more fun than billets. Hornby and I made a serio-comic vow that we would stay there next time.

———— told me to send his regards to the person I was writing to. He is a very nice fellow with a happy gift for amusing phrase, which belies his rather fat and florid appearance.

Tell Margaret that when she has time I expect a detailed account of Cambridge experiences. I wish I had arranged a meeting with the Mozleys.

JACK

8th February 1916

DEAR MOTHER

Many thanks for your letter describing the Dedication. Auntie Mabel sent me a form of the service. It must have been most striking and beautiful.

We did a Battalion route march yesterday, conducted by Hewlett in the absence of higher commanders. A violent stinging shower caught us on the way home and, having halted to put on capes, (long macintoshes) we proceeded looking very strange, as we were wearing packs which bulged out behind. Afterwards the sun came out, very strong and springlike, and the white walls and red tiled roofs shone in a rain washed world. When night came the stars burned like lamps far above the cold wind.

To-day those of us who were done over twelve months ago are being inoculated again. There are far fewer recalcitrants now. The officers are going to a neighbouring village for a lecture from the Brigade Major. To our regret word came along this morning that the rapid wiring competition was a wash-out. We were disgusted, for B's troupe was becoming really a star turn, and I doubt if the other Companies had taken any trouble about it.

I'm not vastly impressed by the " First Hundred Thousand," tho' most of the others are. It was Lumley's copy and has gone the round. Perhaps my palate is jaded, but I think Ian Hay is often rather "hearty," and distinctly so here. There is a masterful chapter ending about a quiet evening in the trenches and the first flare, where he has got it absolutely. (I remember one September morning suddenly realising that the day before had been Sunday). Parts are entirely true to life, and of course there is abundant humour scattered up and down. But the style is often laboriously humorous, don't you think? Need barbed wire produce " excoriations " on people who crawl through it?

I have just been inoculated.

JACK.

9th February 1916

DEAR MOTHER

After my strictures I must pay a tribute to the last chapter of the "First Hundred Thousand"; in those tragic presences the style takes on more dignity and leaves a plain unvarnished tale.

After the inoculation Hammill and I are feeling a little cheap but otherwise flourishing. It was done in the chest this time, and I am going about like a Chelsea pensioner, as the apparent tightness of skin round there keeps me from raising my head properly. The men who were done spent most of the day in blankets.

——— continues to be erratic. He is off somewhere now, and Headquarters are furiously demanding an answer which only he can supply. We went to our lecture yesterday. On our way it poured, and a draggled and overflowing crowd of officers sat in the uncertain lighting of the village school and discussed how to conduct the war.

Meanwhile daylight lingers and Mars shines quite amazingly above the end of the village street. To judge from advertisements in the papers, people in England seem to be spending as much money as ever on motor-cars and what not. The expenditure on clothes too, to judge from *The Tatler* &c., is enormous. Perhaps it is one of the few consolations left in these days.

Have they printed separately Hamilton's Despatch about the Dardanelles? If so would you send it? Would you please thank Father for his neglected offer of knee-pads: they aren't needed as the gum boots we wear in the trenches do the job.

JACK

11th February 1916

DEAR MOTHER

I was sorry to hear of domestic disturbances, and sorry too that Mary has gone. We also have had something of the sort, as the charming youth who is our waiter appeared yesterday as spokesman of a servants' trade union. The claims made by the men's leader were, however, not unreasonable.

We have all quite recovered from inoculation. For a day or two I went about like a veteran colonel wheeled to the window to wave a crutch at Kitchener's troops passing by.

To-day I conducted a fatigue party to ———* to unload coal out of a barge. February is unfortunately proving true to its reputation and performing the celebrated "fill-dyke" act. It rained without a breathing space the whole time we were there. On the whole I think the men were quite amused. Coal brought no doubt a homely feeling to many of them. Some toiled in the holes shovelling coal into baskets, which were handed up by others to more who stood on deck and passed the baskets to others again, who took it along the gang-planks to men with wheel-

*Merville.

barrows, who wheeled it on to a dump. The mid-ships of the barge was incongruously spick and span, and out of a hatch there appeared occasionally the face of a comfortable man or woman, living in evident luxury below. They declared on these appearances that it was " mauvais temps," out of sympathy to the troops. There were dungaree suits for the deck party to protect their uniforms with—a godsend.

I confess I was glad when I saw our relief in the offing. We were all soaked. I of course had a complete change, and the men I find have now got their clothes dried, as we are lucky in having an admirable cook-house which makes a good drying room.

While we were having tea Madame had occasion to come in for something in a cupboard. At somebody's suggestion, she was invited to sit down and have some tea. This delighted the servants intensely, as they are perforce the family's close companions. I saw them one by one take a rapid peep and disappear exploding before I had the door closed. On me I found fell the burden of the conversation. I was happy to be able to offer a piece of Mrs. Borchardt's sponge cake, which pleased Madame and surprised her, as it could be eaten, contrary to apparent expectation, without butter.

I have just finished after a long interval Galsworthy's " Freelands " which Father sent me for my birthday. It is a *really* fine book, I should think the best piece of work he has done.

Barclay is on the staff of a Division still in England, tho' in what capacity I don't know. He is still subaltern rank, I think. Vawdrey I have heard nothing of since they moved South a long while since. I have written to his home for news. I shall write to Mr. Dunn.

JACK

13th February 1916

DEAR MOTHER

We thought to pass away before, but Sunday has found the wheels of our chariots still tarrying ; like the afternoon sun down there in the quiet water meadows, where already there is a ripple of green along the pollard willows.

I went along the canal yesterday to ———* to keep a deferred appointment with Terry, the late M.O. whom I spoke of as leaving, to the general regret, for one of the other Brigades. We met and drank extremely bad tea sitting in the Hotel de Ville, where a big window looks out on the square, with officers' horses tied to the deserted bandstand. We talked long and profitably on States and their proper conduct. I had occasion to call in at Lumley's (C) headquarters on the way back and stayed to supper. He has one or two very nice officers and a capacity of drowning all thought of war in conversational frivolities.

I can't think why we get such unsuccessful Padres. There is such a lot that a good man could do—one with personality and a certain amount of

* Merville

force, and a method too of preaching calculated to appeal to human beings. Intellect isn't needed so much. I do wish we could have a Browne-Wilkinson out here. I suppose it is luck. There must be lots of good fellows about. The R.C. Padre is, of course, a treasure; on leave at present, as a vacancy occurred for the cloth.

Harvey and I went down the road this afternoon to have our photographs taken. We stood in a sort of canvas shed, and a dark man, who badly wanted shaving, performed the deed with most commendable quickness. The C.O. rode past as we were waiting outside and roared with laughter.

I suppose the " vow " you said made you shudder was the idea of staying in the trenches and letting the regiment trek away. And not such a bad idea either, given clean collars and handkerchiefs and moderate opportunities for washing. For the trenches are the most interesting part of the show out here, and not so noisy but one can philosophise there at leisure. One might, too, devise schemes for the better conduct of trench life and warfare, unharassed by regimental duties. As it is, one gets a scrappy blinkered survey of the war, and the work has no continuity.

I too have heard from Teddy. He lives in a world of rumours. We have heard one to-day of a naval nature; nothing in it, I suppose. Your Anti-Zeppelin devices must look weird. Would you send Joe's address again?

JACK

14th February 1916

DEAR MOTHER

We are quite excited now, as casualty officers are coming back to the fold. The Second in Command said to me this morning " Do you know Ridley ?" and Hammill and I nearly tossed our caps in the air on parade, at the thought of our beloved Beatrice radiating upon us again. He reappears shortly; McClinton the Ulsterman came to-day; it is thought that the original captain of C Company is coming also. There has turned up one Voelcker of Rugby, who hailed me by name as I entered the recreation tent this evening, for a lecture from the M.O. We hadn't met before but knew each other by sight. He confirms a notion that Rugby people are good people, tho' I suppose everybody almost can say the same for their schools.

I became aware this morning on parade of general cries of " Mister Hoyle," and turning saw a glittering cavalcade on the meadow that slopes down to a broad backwater skirting our parade ground. It was the C.O. in tow of the Divisional General and a member of his staff. I was asked by the C.O., who acted as interpreter, what the company were doing. I replied that we were at the moment standing easy, as indeed they were, in degagè attitudes and smoking, this being the eleven o'clock break. The question was then shouted across the windy water what we were going to do presently, so I came out with some plausible subjects, and the attention of the gilded company was then called to a platoon of D Company, who were marching badly, and interest in me and my doings lapsed.

Temporarily we have one of our Machine Gun Officers in the mess. It is rather fortunate on the whole that it is temporary. But one musn't cavil behind the firing line.

The " Experiences of a Despatch Rider" is thrilling, and makes the Ian Hay book a poor simpering affair beside it.

JACK

16th February 1916

DEAR MOTHER

This is a great and exciting day. For one thing the winds are tossed about the world, and the ruffled pools in the meadows are blue in the sun's fitful visits, and the interludes of rain are almost the silver showers of April. To walk abroad to-day is to enjoy a symphony, with February's "wild wind-loosened heart" for theme. In this setting our beloved Ridley has just now rejoined us, just the same as ever, one of the most charming people in the world. Finally we are all going back to school again, leaving this inglorious hamlet for historic ground, names to catch the breath at.

There was such a gale this morning that parade became a farce; words of command were inaudible and caps blew in all directions (no doubt human aid was employed by the wilder spirits, under cover of the general boisterous confusion.)

This must be a short letter, as we are in the throes of packing up — I await Margaret's with increasing interest. I trust you will get the photograph ; Harvey is really more attractive than that.

JACK.

17th February 1916

DEAR MOTHER

To-day's march was quite an experience, from the secluded prosperous purlieus of —— to the last stage of all short of the trenches themselves, the deserted fields and crumbling villages just behind the line. Incidentally the march, or part of it, was rather unpleasant, owing to the incompetence of some transport in front of us, whose frequent hesitations and stoppages were very trying to the troops behind. Hornby created some comic relief, as he scornes a valise and carries all his effects on his back, a vast shapeless bundle ; we compare him to the snail carrying her house. What might have been an unfortunate incident occurred at the end of the march. I was with Harvey's platoon and, as we approached Brigade H.Q., we saw a red tabbed officer whom we didn't recognise, standing with our C.O. As there was also a sentry, who ought to present arms to armed parties, I called the platoon to attention, preparatory to giving the sentry eyes right as he performed his obeisance. This he failed to do, being a rather unenterprising and confused looking creature, and I was just beginning a grand remonstrance when I saw the C.O. making violent signals with his crop, and realised that the

Staff Officer was none other than the Divisional General. By this time we were half way past and paid but a hurried homage. It was an absurd incident, but the sort of thing that raises a storm of official fury, as indeed it reflects on a regiment's smartness. But apparently it is blowing over.

We were here once before, but the companies are not in the same billets. B did quite notoriously well last time and is now taking the lowest place. On arrival it was discovered that a table had been pinched; it was here when the Q.M. Sergeant took over earlier this morning; immediately we all cried "the Artillery," who are billeted just across the road. I happened to call in there presently on the strength of a rumour that they had beds to spare, and found our old friends and guests of happy days in the Glory Hole. When the recognition was effected they were hospitality itself and offered any two of us lunch. A few minutes later to my horror I found ——— dashing across the road wild-eyed, ready to burst in and accuse them in no measured terms of bagging our table. This would be an appalling sequel to their kindly invitation, and I found myself positively fending him off at the very door with wide-spread arms, his feelings, the while, fanned by opposition. I got him away from the door but couldn't stop him staring in at the windows. What a scene just behind the firing line of the Great War. Eventually Harvey and I went to lunch. They showed us aeroplane photographs, most enthralling, of the ground just behind the German trenches.

Every now and then there is a terriffic crash from their Battery, and a few seconds later you see the shrapnel burst with a fire-work flash over where the trenches are. The flares of course are always pretty and are tumbling away in twos and threes to-night. Hammill and I have been wandering in the fields, finding and debating on grass-grown relics of forgotten fighting.

Yes, I seem to be permanently in B now.

JACK

19th Februnry 1919

DEAR MOTHER
This is just a note. We are in the trenches again—the cushiest ones conceivable—quite happy, and Olympianly calm. Life moves in measured pace like a clock ; indeed we might be a crowd representing the labour problem under the Ptolemies.

I will write properly the day after to-morrow.

I have just read with the greatest pleasure Margaret's long letter.

JACK

23rd February 1916

DEAR MOTHER
The most trying of serio-comic situations. Just as I am settling down to a snatch of sleep before tea (Hammill snoring the snore of the just near by) the inevitable message comes in—to say, of all

things, that the Brigadier is on his way round. It is public spirited of Vellacott to warn us of the approach of the august cortège. I have warned the sentry to give the alarm at the first scent, and trust the old man will be friendly. But he comes at an ill-chosen hour.

We came into the trenches again last night. Snow had fallen in the afternoon and our arrival suggested Russian scenes.

I am tongue-tied of course by the censorship or would describe our life in detail. We are in historic scenes, among the wrecks of stateliness and beauty, but nowhere near the American University that you suggest.

This is merely to say that I am alive and flourishing and managing to keep warm, as is everybody else.

JACK

P.S.—Could I have " To Rubleben and Back " (Constable). The author came up to Pembroke in my second year and soon won the Jew's prominence. He asked me to write something for a weekly magazine. I produced a longish effort in the Galsworthy manner—it was refused incontinent.

25th February 1916

DEAR MOTHER

My letters are getting scattered again. There is usually lots to say, but when the spare moment comes one's mind recoils from such an effort at the outset.

At present I am monarch of all I survey, living with half one of our platoons in a redoubt, the men, that is, in the dug-outs, I and the three N.C.O's in the ruined farm buildings that adjoin. Our stay is very short, and we can't do all we'd like at improving the place before handing over to others and being no more seen. Given time this would be a very tolerable existence indeed. One can carry out one's own ideas, and seems to live here untroubled of generals or even of colonels.

The snow is lying all about, but the frost seems to have gone. The dark laden figures struggling up to the trenches o' nights are very striking. Every now and then a flare goes up from the front line and transforms the grim and shattered country side. This place is a hub of the universe every evening, a Fleet Street traffic problem of ration parties, reliefs, transport and what not.

I have received the parcel of delectable sweets.

No more woollies are needed at present, thanks very much.

No more now.

I will surely write to Margaret.

JACK

26th February 1916

DEAR FATHER

Many thanks for the puttees, &c.

Although the evidence shows that the Harrod's parcel was beyond doubt for me, I still don't remember ordering "peeled grapes," a Sybarite's repast.

As for books ; that I can't be bothered with them is very far from the case. During our recent long stay in billets there was a certain amount of time for reading, and there developed a sort of circulating library between Vellacott, Lumley, Hewlett and myself. "The Research Magnificent" went the round, and Hewlett devours every novel I get out here long before I do. Somehow I have accumulated an alarmingly big collection, which swells my valise far past the regulation weight. I shall have to begin sending things home. Books about the war are more acceptable than you might suppose. If it wasn't for the number of books I have on hand I would send a list of suggestions. But I must get through more of the stock first.

Arthur's is a great feat. I agree about my signature and have been taking steps lately to make it more legible when the occasion demands.

Just now I have been a sort of Laird over what Shakespeare might call a " pelting farm," which adjoins a redoubt. We have done a little to make the place more defendable. It has been rather fun.

We were much cheered over Erzerum. All honour to the Russians.

JACK

I am not so pessimistic about leave, tho' still not counting on it.

29th February 1916

DEAR MARGARET

As I had so lately received your long letter it was a most particular pleasure to have a second one this evening.

No apology is needed; had there been any omission—which there was not—you have made me divine amends. In any case, as I often leave my best friends for months without a line, I can blame no one else.

I was of course thrilled by your Cambridge letter, and so glad that you met all the old friends. Mrs. Burkitt is marvellous. She moves in a fine spacious atmosphere, symbolised in the easy unmeticulous richness of her drawing room. I was much stimulated too by your picture of the fascinating Miss Boyle. Such accounts are most welcome by their contrast to our surroundings here. They suggest the times before the war, whose pains and labours have faded from memory, so that that life seems as unharrassed as a great river moving amid a drowsy hum of bees, almost as if time was not. Equally certain am I that such an impression is only half true. In Europe there can be no such peace.

Oddly enough, I am writing this from a big clean ward, far from the guns whose crashes shook our billets. *How I come to be here is a long story which must not be told yet awhile. Sitting here (with a slight swelling round the knee) I find the adventure on that night hardly credible.

*The reference is to the affair on account of which he was awarded the Military Cross. The official story is this. "On the "night of 27/28th February 1916, he and Lance-Corporal Hill "made a thorough examination of the enemy wire opposite Neuve "Chapelle, crawling about for three hours. He accurately noticed "the position and number of enemy sentries, and selected a suitable "spot for making the gap in the enemy wire. After returning to our "lines and making his report he guided the party to the selected "spot and covered them whilst the arrangements were being "made. On several occasions Lieut. Hoyle has carried out daring "reconnaissances."

I see I gave a wrong impression of our whereabouts by speaking too excitably of †——— But really †———is rather thrilling; and across the fields, with the opposing hosts between, is that wood which is always something of a mystery, and has seen such bloody passages since the days when the people of the chateau, pausing on the steps from the window to the garden which lie now with tumbled balustrades like a heap of stones, looked across the pleasant fields to the wood's fringe, dark against the grass, and children went doubtless to picnic there. Now it is a military feature of considerable value, and as for the chateau, the communication trench winds in and out skirting the stables, though war has not been so ungentle but you can trace the outlines of the garden and the orchard, with plants still growing and the ghost of a little box-hedge. One likes to reconstruct the life of this place, and speculate what manner of folk they were who peopled these white walls and passed between the round white gate-posts with the ball of stone on top. It is none other than the [1]————that sweeps past the gate-posts, a forlorn wreck of the stately highway that leads on down to [2]————. The faintly mediæval flavour of the place makes one forget that they probably saw the motors of the rich—even if they hadn't one themselves—speed on their way from town to town. Now the trench bursts through the road, and grass almost reaches across it and bricks and tree trunks have fallen on it; and one would venture thereon warily by day for fear of snipers. Now, too, the view of the wood from the big windows the other side of the house is almost blocked by the back view of our trenches just beyond the garden; a thick wall of sandbags with solid buttresses that recalls

[1] Rue du Bois. †Neuve Chapelle. [2] Bethune.

the block-like architecture of Assyrians or Egyptians. Not so the men who have their being there. You should see them in their fur coats. Some of them would not disgrace the wedding of a Cabinet Minister's daughter. Some of the men wear them underneath their jackets, and the coats, fluffing out round their middle, give them a " prehistoric " look.

When I said that they were cushy trenches I was right, for our predecessors had evidently worked on them with consuming zeal, and have left a monument of industry. So that we walk dry shod on boarded ways. The frost, too, didn't seem to bother us, nor was the snow nearly deep enough to be inconvenient. Indeed our troubles are not what those at home imagine; for one thing the year has turned and the waters are receding.

To-night they will go up to the trenches and I shall not be with them. In fancy I follow their progress, dark silent processions on the road's broken surface, and the stealthy advance into the trenches in a world that answers the falling lights with sudden brilliance and racing shadows. Only it is usually not as stealthy as it should be, and one has continually to rush along and appeal with curses to some one's common sense (which they will never learn, as they have never yet suffered—*unberufen*—for the lack of it). Glad as I am of a rest I should rather like to be there and see it all out. Besides it means more work for Hammill.

I am so glad you are meeting interesting people. Please give my love to the Vicarage folk.

JACK

1st March 1916

DEAR MOTHER

You will be pleased to hear that I am not going up with them to the trenches to-night, for the simple reason that I am sitting in a roomy ward in ——* with something called bursitis about my left knee. I think I must have knelt on a loose piece of barbed wire the other night, tho' I felt nothing at the time. But the next day I reported to the M.O. with a rather swollen knee. He made me spend yesterday in bed, and to-day I set off in a motor ambulance. We drove away from the shattered houses—mere heaps some of them of sodden straw and rubble—to the comparative miracle of a town. Here I was met by a friendly R.A.M.C. Captain, and while my knee was being looked at, a fine old boy came in, middle-aged and opulent. A glance at my leg and he rattled out a diagnosis different from our M.O.'s, adding the word bursitis; the quickness and confidence with which he did this impressed me enormously.

Bursitis appeared to involve my immediate transference to ——*, so I got into the ambulance again and drove here through country that seemed Utopianly prosperous. Life here is very serene. I believe the place was a hospital before. It is nice to see and talk to the English Sisters. An agreeable quiet prevails in these rooms and we only speak to each other when the spirit moves us.

JACK

* Merville.

2nd March 1916

DEAR MOTHER

To-day finds me sitting up in a dressing-gown, as I have no slacks, and puttees would be a nuisance when my knee has to have hot fomentations several times daily. I hardly feel it now.

I'm afraid you will have formed awful pictures of perilous escapades culminating in a wound; but it was merely a patrol,* entirely unbeknownst to the Hun who stamped his cold toes or hummed the Court of Luxembourg Waltz all the time; and the injury was unconscious.

There are no serious cases here. I am sitting next a Birdman, who is doing a jig-saw puzzle (an indifferent occupation of such precious leisure, though perhaps an antidote for the strain of his job) with the help of an agreeable A.S.C. man. In bed are a gunner with bronchitis practically over; an unknown subaltern with exhaustive knowledge of the movements of the entire army as it seems; the Transport Officer of the ———, an unattractive and bibulous creature I fear; someone whose unconscious grace in walking comes from the Florentines or the ancients, and is a great pleasure; and two doctors, which seems wrong. Breakfast in bed is of course quite an exquisite luxury, and there are pretty bits of assorted china they serve things up on. I have all the books I want and life goes on very pleasantly.

No, I'm afraid there is no chance of leave at present.

JACK

* See Note to letter of 29th Feb.

4th March 1916

DEAR FATHER

Is not the 7th your birthday? This is to greet you, and may it be the last under such conditions.

March is coming in like a lion, with rain and now snow, and I am a lucky dog to be sitting cosy here in a dressing gown, with no duties, while the others pursue their normal course. To-day as a matter of fact the Regiment is out resting in their ruined billets; it is a pretty fair rest, though short, for the nearness of the trenches consigns you to almost complete inactivity, and enforces the regulations of the Conventicle Act.

My knee is very nearly well, and I can walk without noticing it, though I haven't had an opportunity of putting the walls of this place behind me.

I see they have had an Economy Meeting in London. My opinion, drawn from advertisements and the illustrateds, is that most people are spending quite as much as ever on *e.g* motor-cars, clothes (women at any rate), jewels, lunch, &c.; and that the war has not really shaken people's habits in spite of all they have heard about it. It may be a one-sided view, and the pictures in the papers not representative. I keep thinking tho', what a different spectacle we as a nation must offer from the Athenians in their Great War.

JACK

5th March 1916

DEAR MOTHER

This afternoon I came back to the world again. It has been a delightful holiday.

The day began quite deliciously, as I finished a novel in bed and wrote a long letter to Gilbert; later I went out for a walk as the weather was inviting ; indeed it was quite a lovely day of early Spring. I went past our old billets outside the town and turned in at one of them, where the people are very kind. Monsieur, a most charming old gentleman, who wanders round clock-mending, I think, was extremely cordial. Madame, who is hardly his equal but very nice too, (she once cured the bleeding of my nose by making me sit with my feet in a tub of hot water) jabbered away like one possessed. Altogether it was a very pleasant rencontre and we exchanged various reminiscences of others of our officers who have lodged there. A bottle of wine was also broached, and in deference to some native custom I had to have two glasses, otherwise I should have had to hop away on one leg. On the way back I was hailed by a fellow who was with us at Camberley and was attending another such school of instruction in ——— now. He carried me off to lunch with some of the pupils and spoke with regret and feeling of Billy.

After that it was time to go to the motor ambulance, and I had a jolly drive. There was a very pleasant meeting with Hammill who hadn't expected to see me back so soon. I learnt to my surprise that we weren't going into the trenches for a day or two; I had reckoned that we were due to-night, and had excited the sympathy of the Sister by telling her my destination.

I received another parcel of sweets this evening, also the Ruhleben book for which I had asked. Very many thanks.

May I have another pair of gloves on a tape. Mine got absolutely ruined the other night; also a few decent pencils, Kohinoor or the like.

You will have seen Jones' name in the casualty list. It was only a touch and he walked and talked quite unconcernedly afterwards. I hear he is now at Nice.

JACK

8th March 1916

DEAR MOTHER

Now fades the last long streak of snow, and I for one am not sorry to see it. For though the night's snow-storm transformed this most desolate corner of the world, and indeed made the prettiest pictures when the lights went up, there is no doubt that snow does not commend itself in the trenches. But it is now melting off under the March sun, which makes the view from the dug-out entrance quite radiant. Hammill and I live here, Harvey and —— (returned from a short absence, more of a rolling stone than ever) at the other end of the Company line. This dug-out, except for the lowness of the roof is rather nice, and has two bunks one above the other as in a ship ; —— is now stretched on the upper one grunting and snoring most brutishly.

As for this corner of the world—picture what probably was once a piece of flat meadow land, now absolutely broken up by a formless tangle of trenches all disused and half full of water; the vestiges of grass almost smothered by the up-turnings of clay; against the sky behind are a scraggy line of broken-spirited trees and the wrecks of ——*.

Mrs. Borchardt is really to be congratulated on her latest effort; the cake I received two days ago is a work of genius.

Harvey two others and I have received a communication from the Divisional General congratulating us on a piece of work the other night—the night I hurt my knee.

The oddest little shy gunner is forward-observing here to-day and messes with us; he never " utters" till spoken to and then only in the briefest compass.

JACK

11th March 1916

DEAR MOTHER

I'm afraid it will be a great disappointment to you that I should be back again so soon. But it was well worth it.

We saw more warfare yesterday than we have seen for some time, tho' of course that is not saying much. I am glad to say that the Company is still intact after it. It was quite exhilarating to hear our shrapnel swish over our heads; the reply was the same, if not so agreeable.

* Neuve Chapelle.

Winter's departure is rather malicious, but we contrive to keep warm, and it is pleasant to think that the warm days are soon coming.

In haste for the Post.

JACK

13th March 1916

DEAR MOTHER

The world seems to have changed in the last few days ; for Spring has come and we are out of the trenches.

We left on Saturday night; the weather had been milder during the day, at which we all rejoiced. I speak of this particular night because of the light it throws on ———. The latter now feels the loss of his ancient freedom quite desperately, and his unsuitability for a life in which uncongenial calls are continually made on him. Shortly before the relief was due he came along and said he was going for a walk between the lines. This was most inconvenient at such a moment, invoking as it did a warning of all sentries, when one had other things to think about. In spite of my entreaties I learnt later that he had darted out unaccompanied ; but he was soon back. All went peaceably until the relief was in progress, when suddenly one of our sergeants came hurtling down the line ordering sentinels not to fire, as Mr. ——— was out. Full of indignation I went along to the left. There I was told an incredible tale, but mounting on to the fire-step I was forced to believe my eyes. There, away beyond the dark shapes of a line of pollard willows that march towards our trench, was the light of an electric torch swinging round and round as if held at arms length. Our men were explaining to their relievers that —— was just like that. In spite of indignation and anxiety, gazing out at the light swinging round somewhere in front of the German wire, I couldn't help rejoicing at someone who for a moment had ragged the whole show. —— was in presently. He had been sitting in Harvey's dug-out, and hearing a German machine-gun and feeling fed-up and bored, rushed out vowing he would bomb the thing. According to his account, he found the Germans talking hard; he hurled some abusive taunts, and absolute silence followed. The odd thing is that he was never fired on. Indeed he seems to bear a charmed life, for he is always exposing himself absurdly.

That incident closed, and we wormed our way out among the gaunt looming shattered walls of ——* and out along the road, with the thought of bullets less and less imminent, towards buildings more complete.

I must stop now, as it is late enough for me to be able to turn out the guard for the last time, and after that I must go to bed.

Enough for the present that we seem to be in a new world.

JACK

*Neuve Chapelle.

14th March 1916

DEAR MOTHER

At the moment I don't regret at all having left hospital.

Last time I told of——'s efforts. The edge was rather taken off our return that night by rumours of a move further back on the morrow, and the prospect of sitting up, waiting for orders. All the same our room in that deserted cottage seemed very cheering. ——— too, in his capacity of Sniping Officer, had brought an imitation head ; this had been put on one of the beds, and some clothes cunningly disposed ; accordingly when, coming in after the others, I heard that we had a new subaltern who had misbehaved badly and was now lying in a drunken torpor, the glassy stare of the face was quite convincing, and it took me several minutes to see through a very realistic make-up.

I shan't easily forget the next morning. We had just come in from a period in the trenches rather tougher than usual, during which departing winter had had a rare fling ; the damp and cold and squalor and lack of sleep had produced an effect ; and that morning when I stepped out of that decaying cottage it was to a subdued radiance of sunshine and blue sky. The snow and the cold gone like a dream, everything fresh and full of happy promise, even those forlorn abandoned outskirts of the war smiling, it seemed literally another world; as if, the night before, we had left more than the trenches ; and there came to one the triumphant realisation of Spring, broken through winter's defences, and bringing just that reassuring sense of something strong, permanent, unchanging, beside which high explosive, that shatters these villages to brick-dust and drives away their moving spirit, appeared as the transitory impertinence it is.

Then follows, after hustling preparations, the march here in real warmth that made us feel our packs. And you can imagine what it is like, after the trenches and their attendant weather of those few days, to wander about here in Spring sunshine with the buds thick on tree and hedge, and after the alarms and excursions cf the war, to watch the immemorial life of home and farm carrying almost unconcernedly on.

JACK

17th March 1916

DEAR MOTHER

I am happy to think that the incident of the other night, mixed as its result was for us, has been able to give you pleasure. The communication in question was merely sent round to each of us (four) and had to be returned. As far as I remember it was something like this—" The Major General desires to express to these officers his appreciation of their courage and devotion to duty, and especially of the excellent reconnaissance made by Lt. Hoyle at *———on the night......on the occasion of the attempted raid on the enemy's trenches, which was well planned and deserved to be successful." I still maintain that I had the cushy part of the show, as it was my job to retire discreetly before the scrapping, and that Harvey had the nerve-racking part. Also they made me out to be much

* Neuve Chapelle

cleverer than I really was. Some day I will tell you all about it and the tragic denouement (tho' no one was even scratched) that in a moment wrecked hours of successful preparation. But not yet.

I am always intending to get a decent letter off, but even in billets one seems to be quite revoltingly busy. I am just in now from a wiring party, and the cocks are already crowing.

We have moved a mile or two in the last twenty-four hours, and for the first time out here are billetted actually in a town, with the cookers drawn up in the square.

On Wednesday night I was omitted accidentally by the M.O., who wrote the invitation to dine at H.Q., and bethought me that it was an opportunity to ask in Philip Abraham, whom I could swear I had seen as we were marching in. He was perfectly charming of course. I liked hearing an Abraham voice again.

The weather is wonderful, and these balmy nights vividly recall night-operations at Clevedon.

I have a steel helmet, but don't feel extraordinarily enthusiastic about the breast-plate. Will you thank Father for the gloves, which are capital.

Gilbert works now at Haxby Road Hospital, York, but says he expects to be sent out somewhere soon. The parcel was from him.

JACK

19th March 1916

Dear Mother

Life does seem different just now. After the cold and snow and mud and dreary skies, to linger in this sleepy country town where even the March winds have dropped, and the nights are like the nights of Summer !

I think the men simply love being in a town again, tho' as they say they wish it was St. Helens. Meanwhile for us the change is almost incredible. Last night when I had dined quietly and pleasantly with Lumley and his nice subaltern Hopkins, Ridley looked in and after that we seemed to wander about for the best part of two hours under the pretence of seeing each other to bed. In the silent moon-flooded streets we might have been in Cambridge, in the silence that follows the close of college gates at ten ; the clock of the Hotel de Ville was faintly reminiscent of the exquisite new chimes of Caius ; back-waters of the canal might have been the landing stage by Queen's, and the sound of a staff-car approaching was like the mail motor bus that I have heard a hundred times roaring down Pembroke Street, and furiously changing gear as it turned the corner towards the giant trees and the nightingales of the Trumpington Road.

There is one place here where the canal winds alongside the cobbled street, and beyond the bridge is a small island thick with saplings and the tower of an old windmill behind. Wrapped in silence and silvered with the steady moonlight this spot is almost incredibly beautiful, merely by contrast, doubtless, with what is here only a very few miles off. So, pretending to see each other to bed, we stood entranced at this and other scenes, scarcely able to believe in what we return to in a few days' time.

The other night, before we came on here, Hammill Lumley and I had an extraordinarily nice dinner party at the beloved Ridley's, and a superb discussion followed on war, quite like old times, with everyone contributing something to an idea tossed to and fro.

JACK

HOTEL MEURICE
35 RUE VICTOR HUGO
BOULOGNE-SUR-MER
*SUNDAY 3rd April 1916

DEAR MOTHER

Here we are in civilization—according to this world's standards—still, as the train doesn't go till mid-day to-morrow. I half suspected, and I confess secretly looked forward to some such delay. They frequently occur. The troops are up in the camp while we dally down here.

It has been really hot, rather overpowering as the first heat always is. I went to see Jeannie Abraham; first at the hospital, quite beautifully set out inside, where she was not, then at a hotel where they retire to ; she was out and I left a note ; later in the afternoon I was surprised and pleased to see her here where she

* On the way back after his last home leave.

looked in on her way to church, accompanied by a less distinctive colleague. She made affectionate enquiries after all of you. I thought of going to see Kitty, but the distance according to the map is greater than I had expected.

It was a lovely ten days, wasn't it? And fittingly ended by that exquisite play. The weather too this morning took the edge off departure. We breakfasted very pleasantly in the train, gliding among forests of hop-poles through the undulating country. Waiting for the boat to start we watched the gulls, delighted as they wheeled and swooped and squabbled over tit-bits. As we stood out to the fresh breeze and the haze our destroyer forged alongside, sometimes drawing ahead, and then dropping back and racing across our stern, just like a dog.

The hotels here are good in parts and shabby in others. The crowd in the streets is I suppose bourgeois, unattractive on the whole.

I left my map on your desk in the hall; would you send this when you reach home.

Love to the Aunts.

JACK

4th April 1916

DEAR MOTHER

After our soothing stay at the port of arrival we made a historic journey yesterday, the day beginning with a late breakfast at our hotel and ending in the trenches, amid a restive crackle of rifles. The weather was incomparable, and, from finishing " Prince Otto" in the mild sunlight of the courtyard at the hotel, to curling up for a few hours sleep in this dug-out, it was quite a memorable series of experiences.

The sun glared on the platform, where the train seemed to have taken root, until we moved out three-quarters of an hour behind time. We were delighted meanwhile with the very complete and comfortable fitting up of a spick and span hospital train on the other side. The journey was a series of delights—first through rolling foothills richly green with spring and strewn with daisies; children playing in the fields were the finishing touch to scenes that bore no suggestion of war. Later, in the mellower hours of afternoon, the colours had the intensity of pre-Raphaelite paintings. We glided through fens where every straight lane of water had its rustic boat, like a gondola of unknown antiquity, loaded with dried rushes. The peasants stopped in their leisurely toil to watch us, old women with sun-bonnets mostly; the whole picture had the radiance of full summer. Our progress was slow, and many of the troops sat perched on the foot-boards. Gradually we came to familiar fields with the evening mists rising, and in a magical warm twilight, alive with the lovely scents of the earth, we glided into railhead.

But I must now catch the post.

JACK.

5th April 1916

Dear Mother

I told how we arrived at——at dusk. Here anti-climax intervened, for there was no transport to meet us. Oddly enough, on coming down to breakfast that morning we had met the Adjutant, Hammill, and the R.C. padre on their triumphant way to England, and had been told we should be met. Eventually however the well-known cart rolled up and we jogged very pleasantly along through a most beautiful evening a-glitter with stars ; the eastern horizon tremulous with Verey lights and the flashes of unheard guns. Every house and bend of the road had its associations. So we came to the transport lines and the Tranport Officer's billet, where we had supper and heard regimental gossip. Then on again to the ruined parts, up to the limit for wheeled traffic. This was indeed a contrast we thought, as we dropped flat in occasional flurries of machine gun bullets.

We found the C.O. and Adjutant at H.C. in good spirits, and after frivolous conversation rejoined our Companies.

Now we are in the ruined houses again ; under the hands of their occupants these become quite habitable places.

It consoles me for coming back to be getting your letters again.

Jack

8th April 1916

DEAR MOTHER

I'm afraid my correspondence has broken down absolutely. My brain is becoming addled with company-commanding, an occupation I detest. There seems to be no time to settle down to write decently.

It is a perfectly lovely Spring day, and hardly any distance at all behind the trenches the hedges are resplendent. In fact it is quite absurd to think there is a war on. This billet is now looking quite respectable, as the walls were this morning draped, Liberty-fashion, with sacking.

JACK.

13th April 1915

DEAR MOTHER

It is awful to think how you must have waited for a line lately, but you do understand that it was not intentional on my part.

I hope however to make up now. It is as if a veil had lifted. You see I had only one officer, and he inexperienced and placid, for ——, nominally mine, is of course out of the question. There was a lot to get done, and I was in an absurdly distrait mood, with appalling results and a consciousness of continually running after trains that had started hours before So that I moved in a sort of nightmare and became a positive byword. The clouds lifted somewhat the afternoon before we left the trenches, and when we got out and settled round a scratch meal in the room we had improved so much last time by papering the walls with sacking, I suddenly felt there was nothing more to worry about, and have been a different man since.

A distinctly bright spot lately has been the Battery officers. One was our guest each day this time. The most exciting day for me was when a rather studious looking gunner in spectacles turned up—I had just dropped quite a bad brick, and his comments were a little brusque I thought. It is amusing to recall how that conversation developed. We pottered among platitudes and got on to the subject of ———. He then began tying me down to clear definitions with great intellectual zeal, and, though he touched on chords that thrilled me rather, I was still slightly ruffled and on my guard. A casual mention of Raemeker, in the course of sheer gossip, definitely turned the conversation into certain channels, but I was still treating his criticisms as opinionated and upstart. By imperceptible degrees I realised that the defensive was not called for, rather the ever open door, and thereafter we scaled heights and plumbed depths of philosophy, till it was with sudden astonishment that I realised we had been strangers an hour ago.

No more for the moment.

JACK

16th April 1916

DEAR MOTHER

I believe I have deserted you again. The times have been strenuous enough. Now we are back again in untroubled realms, and as one looked across the sun-baked plough-land this afternoon the only suggestion of war was the silly old balloon over ———.

I wrote of being much harassed by affairs, but they have vanished, as I think I said. Now, too, Hammill is back.

We came to-day from our ruins—but we had improved our surroundings considerably (indeed I think that after the war I shall have a room papered with sacking)—to farms in the neighbourhood of *———, and it seems quite wonderful to be talking French again. The sun is getting strong now, and it was quite a hot march to-day.

I must go to bed, as we may have another early start in the morning.

JACK.

17th April 1616

DEAR MOTHER

We are now in the place where we stayed such a long time two months ago. Little has happened here in the meantime except that the grass is a more

*Merville

vivid emerald, and there are splashes of quite gorgeous green along the village street. The divisional band has been playing in a field ringed in by the usual rapt crowd, and hearing it in the offing one felt that we were back in the middle of peace-training.

A mounted officer looked at me just now with a tentative expression which I ignored, thinking him as a matter of fact, in the half light, a rather sorry fellow. Later he passed again and this time turned and greeted me by name. He proved to be one of our Pembroke bloods, from the Ivy Court galaxy, a very nice fellow indeed. He is a sapper attached to the gunners, with rather a good job. We talked about the last two Pembroke balls.

It is extremely pleasant seeing the natives in their haunts again. Our resting place last night was excellent. The old lady where we messed was rather cold at first, but warmed to us rapidly. Here we are all in our original billets, among old friends who hailed us with shouts on arrival. To-day, when I broke a glass dome which enclosed a mixed collection of imitation fruit mounted as a sort of set piece, Madame's chief comment was that it was well it wasn't my leg that was broken.

Hewlett is at present acting C.O. and strafes companies unmercifully. Ridley plays adjutant to his colonel, and is the most charming of adjutants conceivable, combining efficiency with kindness and a helping hand all round, most unusual phenomena.

As for birds singing, you may hear larks any morning rising unconcernedly over the actual trenches. In the ghost of a willow that stands out of the parapet I heard a thrush the other evening, as if it was in the garden at home. I was struck particularly one morning ; at dawn, while some of us were threading our way along the communication trench as it meanders in and out the broken walls and trampled gardens of *——, at one corner where you break through the road there was a robin warbling peacefully, as if its surroundings were entirely normal. And it was in the intervals of the cracks of a German machine gun that one heard it. In that place we had primroses, gathered perilously from the chateau garden, in boxes at the door of the mess dug-out, admired of all the passers by.

That last period in the trenches ends in a vision of our shrapnel, bursting with a flash in the half light of dawn, against a sky in which a long band of pale crimson merging into dove grey was drawn behind the dark tracings of the wood opposite. "Iron rations" said one of the men as a heavy shell burst somewhere behind the enemy line.

The weather varies very much ; on the whole it isn't as warm as it might be for the time of year. Thanks very much for the khaki handkerchief. The sponge cake arrived to-day.

JACK

* Neuve Chapelle

20th April 1916

DEAR MOTHER

To-day we are in very different scenes, among country lanes that wander up and down shaded in their now flourishing hedges, and from windy up-lands we get great views of fields and roads and farms and churches stretching away to faint blue hills. In places it is just like Yorkshire, in others one sees exact replicas of bits of Salisbury Plain. The showers of the season sweep over us, and wild violets and wood anemones are bright in the sunshine that follows. So that this morning we might have been at Clevedon. At the end of afternoon parade I heard one of the men say that all the days ought to be like that. I think it bucks them all up to be able to look about them again.

Here we seem worlds away from the war ; not a sound of it reaches us, and these sequestered villages with their few unsophisticated shops bring no suggestion of battlefields that all Europe watches. It has become hard to remember that we were in the trenches a few days back, among grim shattered houses and roads hardly recognizable.

They have a charming architectural fashion here ; the aged red-brick of these farms is streaked with broad courses of white stone. The effect is entirely unlike the new quad at Rugby though that also has streaks.

In weather I fancy we are doing rather better than you, for tho' it is chilly o' nights the April sun is warm between the showers.

JACK

21st April 1916

DEAR MOTHER

I have just received the beautiful handkerchiefs and the Perugino card. Very many thanks.

The divisional band, a great acquisition, is playing in the village school popular songs, musical comedy, and what not reminiscent of Old England. It is odd to hear the music sounding over an alien land.

We spend our day on a high plain like Blackdown Ridge; on one side the green land undulates, ending in a long row of Noah's Ark trees lining the crest of a ridge; on the other the country is like the chess-board landscape in " Through the Looking Glass " with ——* and its dominating towers in the centre, and round and beyond that plough and meadow and village stretching away to a faint blue line of hills.

The farm where we mess is dirty and poverty-stricken, having fallen on evil days, as one would judge from a certain dignity in its design and the species of Adam fire-place in this large empty room. Hammill and I sleep however in great comfort in the scrupulously clean house of a shrivelled dame who has pieces of good furniture, and lives in constant dread of a fire breaking out on the premises. Our cigarettes give her shivers of apprehension. We have a large light airy room with big windows that open properly.

This morning some of us were made to shake in our shoes. An important officer is attached to us at present, and has the platoon officers and sergeants out

*Aire.

every morning for drill. We quake in fear of a reproof for inefficiency in doing what we are supposed to make other people do. It was the most terrifying situation I have known since school.

It is quite warm between the showers.

JACK

22nd April 1916

DEAR MOTHER

Please don't worry any more about my doings, as that rather trying period is over. I have "got shut of it," as the Company Quarter-Master Sergeant says.

My spectacled gunner was one of the Divisional gunners, and so of the same status as myself. Our conversation was a curious oasis in that tour of the trenches.

———— is at present curled up in his sleeping sack on the top of the dresser, while the rest of us are just beginning dinner. He is as erratic as ever. They have given him the Scouts to keep him quiet. He rather touched me the other day. We stood in the sunk lane that winds up the hill behind the farm here, and he suddenly said how he longed for freedom, in the most heart-felt way, in utter disregard of the fresh April beauty breaking so lavishly round us in the hedges and slanting coppices.

It has rained without a moment's respite all day.

JACK

25th April 1916

DEAR MOTHER

Thanks so much for the Easter egg. The greetings I received included chocolates from Mrs. Hewlett.

We are having halcyon weather : real heat beats down on our high parade ground ; and under skies of amazing stars ———— and I pitch our nightly camp. A sleeping bag inside a valise makes a perfect bed. I put mine beside two tall trees and look up along their trunks from where I lie ; in the morning, walking a few yards up the slope over the dewy undergrowth, I come on ————— among the saplings lying like a mummy, and all his wordly goods round him. He has taken now to disappearing altogether of an afternoon.

We mind our " p's " and " q's " in these days, to avoid passages with our Staff Officer attached as second in command and general gingerer up all round. The C. O. is simply out-Heroded. The result is all for the good I think.

You should see our morning parades. At the dinner hour the cookers and most of the transport arrive accompanied by a varied train of cooks and what not. Footballs are also brought. The band strikes up and gives to the whole a Margate beach flavour. The officers lunch serenely in sequestered groups, until everybody is hauled up, as yesterday, for a wild football fantasia in which hundreds take part and only dribbling is allowed. Further manœuvres are carried out after the interval, and by the end of the afternoon we are exhausted but not ill content.

Ritson has rejoined us after his long absence. We have several new officers now ; there was quite a batch of new faces when I got back from leave. On the whole they are a great improvement as regards certain features we have discussed. Trinity is represented by two pleasant people. There are two new subalterns in the Company,—— who is normal and very nice, and ——a quaint creature with a decorous and placid manner, who likes to diffuse an atmosphere of a Byronic and licentious past ; the impression he leaves however is so gentle and nebulous that we all rather laugh at him. He is reputed to have shot a man in a duel, and he affects in his mild way to be a connoisseur of wines.

Would a kettle be a difficult thing to send out here ? We badly need one for the mess, but if they are hard to send by post I will try and get one here. It shouldn't be as large as the big one in the kitchen at home, but a normal size for the second brew of tea for five or six thirsty folk.

I do hope your flag day yesterday was a success.

JACK

27th April 1916

DEAR MOTHER

Please excuse my not writing yesterday, but we were on the run all day, and there was no time for a letter besides various other details that ought not to have been left undone.

We all went to bathe yesterday. After doing a certain amount of ordinary training we marched off and landed up at a coal-pit head, after a much longer journey than we had expected, in absolute summer heat. Situated as it was in a pretty valley our mine, with its chimneys and high slag-heap and railway lines, suggested the vale of Hinnom on the way to Buxton and similar scenes. The owner had apparently built excellent baths for his employes. On the way we passed a chateau so enchanting that I almost deserted. It came right out of a fairy-story. A central wing, of exquisite proportion, in grey stone with Tudor (?) windows and a slate roof, was flanked by round towers with narrow windows and various irregular features like over-hanging balconies. The towers ended as minarets, and other towers in different styles pricked up from different corners. The castle stood among its trees in sun-warmed fields strewn with daisies. Ladies in brocades and pointed hats would have been no surprise.

The weather is as I say summery to a degree. The parkin cake received with thanks.

JACK

27th April 1916

DEAR MOTHER

These days are so strenuous and spent in such heat that there is little opportunity or inclination for letter-writing.

Last night we carried out some manœuvres, a night advance towards a certain point. The kick-off was unforgettable. The discipline was faultless, complete silence being maintained, but chaos set in in regard to direction—we all strayed across each other's front, with whispered recriminations between the officers. Representatives of the most unexpected companies turned up continually, and we all straggled forward like driven leaves before a shifting wind, faintly trusting that all would come right in the end. A feature of the whole was the tumultuous and incessant croaking of frogs, whose chorus filled the magical April night with exactly the noise, as I remembered with pleasure and amusement, of Aristophanes' *brek-ek-ek-ek-co'ax-co'ax*. They seemed a mocking comment on our bewildered and floundering evolutions. We untied the knots at last and carried on in proper style. In some trees on the edge of the hill I was delighted to hear a nightingale. It was an added beauty to the lovely night. Only once before had I heard one, in the great trees of the Trumpington Road, and thought how it sounded in the English air like a voice from the warm South.

Further evolutions to-day in remarkable heat, and great things to-morrow. The gingering-up process continues.

I have had letters from Father which I will acknowledge presently.

JACK

28th April 1916

DEAR MOTHER

Never have I seen Spring come with so sweeping and triumphant an onset. Perhaps it is always the same in countries south of England. At any rate we are sweltering now, manœuvring daily on the undulating land with its parched soil and dusty roads.

There were operations on a biggish scale to-day. Last evening I was suddenly called upon to draw on the school blackboard a sketch of the morrow's area, enlarging from a small sketch map. Though I was rather pressed for time it was quite fun, and I had put some sort of representation on the board when the audience began to drop in for the C.O.'s lectures.

To-day we carried out the scheme accordingly. At the end a vast crowd of assorted officers assembled for the pow-wow. After the Brigadier and certain Colonels had justified themselves the Major-General made some remarks, very sound and well thought out, and with such coolness and dignity of manner that I was quite captivated and thought him a very fine gentleman indeed.

Now for my bed under the trees.

JACK

3rd May 1916

DEAR MOTHER

I was delighted to receive the second Aunt Sarah production. I hadn't touched a book for days and days, and the style (for, whatever one thinks about their purport, both the books have style) was extremely refreshing.

Strange doings in the outer world. To us in our rural retreat, where every day the sloping meadows are a richer green and brighter with daisies, and the nightingales sing in the warm scented nights, events in Dublin are extraordinary.

It seems to have been a time of high pressure, exciting events crowding together.

We too have had quite stirring times with our Brigade field-days. Tho' the gingering up process is less definite after the departure to his own sphere of the chief exponent, the influence remains.

We make an early start with a longish dusty march in the increasing heat. Every day we pass my castle, the joyous embodiment of work well done. Then there is the pause before the battle on some grassy down that the light wind fans, followed by the battle itself. On one of these occasions I was given a special job on which a good deal hinged, and made the most appalling blunder conceivable ; the discovery of which made my flesh creep and mind reel with visions of the brigade, irretrievably mixed up, trying to untie the knot at the cost (under actual conditions) of frightful carnage ; colonels swearing, the Major General dancing on the horizon, and withering comments at the subsequent pow-wow. As it happened, my arrangements had been completely ignored by the regiment whose cynical disregard of them saved the situation ; and my *faux pas* would never have been noticed if I had not rushed up to the C.O. to explain it, in hopes of mitigating the approaching outbreak. The C.O. however said nothing and all went well.

The operations end with shouting and tumult against a background of gold braid and scarlet. An uncertain pause follows ; then the officers' call, and we gather round the General, while the troops sweep past under N.C.O's towards dinner, frantically warned in undertones as they approach not to disturb the Olympians by shouted obeisances. The Brigadier says his say, the Colonels make explanations, and our Major General, in faultless breeches and leggings, adds a final word always cool and dignified. The council ends, and we drift off in twos and threes in the wake of the men, who when we reach them in some sequestered spot are well on with dinner. At the last of these meetings I met my gunner acquaintance of *——.

We find the troops in a shady reach of the road or on some sequestered slope, and spend a hot quarter-of-an-hour shepherding them from forbidden sources of water, which attract them like flies. Then very thirsty and glad to sit down, we extract our lunch from the cooker (on one occasion one of the two bottles of *vin rouge du pays* had broken and, besides making the bag look disgusting, it left one for the six of us) and retire behind a bush, from which we eye other folk's lunches. After a rather disturbed siesta the whistle blows, and so home through the dust and mellow heat of the golden afternoon, winding among the rolling fields of young corn, by the blossoming hedges, past the fairy castle and the ruined solitary windmill, a tower on the open down, to the last gentle descent where the grey spire gleams among the rich radiant trees, to a very welcome tea. And then heigh ho ! for to-morrow's scheme.

* Neuve Chapelle

We were out all Sunday night and carried out quite a successful operation. The pause before battle was remarkable. For a long time we stood crowded and waiting in a sunk lane, and all the time in a tree a few yards away a nightingale was singing. The contrast between it amongst the leaves and us going into action inevitably recalled Keats. When we moved on we still heard it, until we became involved in further stages of the advance. We lay out there on the broad flat top of a hill, while " dawn's left hand was in the sky," the troops getting rather cold and restless. Later the Brigadier came along, a grotesque silhouette against the faint sky. We did much the same thing last year, just after I came back from Camberley, and I remembered that then as now, at a certain stage of morning's coming, the sky became suddenly filled with lark-song, when the moment before there was not a sound. The shapes of things grew distinct and faces recognizable, and at last we were allowed to talk and wander about. Operations ended and, it being now daylight, the cookers rolled up with tea. Hornby had in no time made himself a fire with straw pulled from a stack. He Bowles and Jones had behaved quite scandalously while we were supposed to be lying unperceived ready to spring. Bowles, with routing and scuffling, had pulled down straw and wrapped himself up in it. Hornby lay there too talking, and Jones, who had joined the party, created disturbances in cynical disregard of the situation. Then, after tea and snacks, the march home, all of us a little bleary about the eyes, while " the still morn went out with sandals grey," and delicate spires of cottage smoke stole up straight in the still air until the sun, up long before, rolled over a hill in full strength, and by the time we passed the castle we were in summer heat again. We got in about eight o'clock to breakfast, and learned that nothing would happen for some hours, which produced a delicious holiday feeling. After breakfast an unusual silence fell on the village. While Hammill slept I had a glorious lingering wash; in the village square, which our fine big windows command, hardly a thing moved, and there was no sign of life throngh the open windows of the Mairie, where two companies of officers mess. I spent the morning on the wooded slope where we sleep; I intended to write home, but of course fell asleep, and woke with a fierce sun beating on me, to find the morning gone.

Enough for the moment.

JACK.

May 4—Just in from a long day and an early start to-morrow.

5th May 1916

DEAR MOTHER

Do you remember about —— who was head of the house at Rugby, that unhappy time? I saw the other day that he had got the Military Cross and was much excited.

It is stewing hot. We had another large-scaled affair yesterday; a very important personage was present but made no observation. To my unspeakable amazement the C.O., when the Brigadier asked for names, detailed me for the same job that I bungled so appallingly last time. I had a rather amusing day, with passages with a colonel in the other brigade, who acted in defiance of orders and truculent scorn of my entreaties. We didn't get in till dusk.

I have sent a few more things home, including my British Warm which I packed with tears; but my valise was quite scandalously too heavy, as the C.O. found the other day when all our valises were weighed, mine heading the list, almost three times the regulation weight.

JACK

8th May 1916

DEAR MOTHER

We are installed in our pastures new and well pleased with them.* I feel that this is the France indeed : our old haunts were of course slightly mongrelly. We passed this morning through the town I laboriously described yesterday, but we are now out of convenient walking distance from it, which is rather a pity. This village is as charming as one could wish, with white walls and blossoming orchards and gardens full of flowers such as we never saw round ——, and which delight the heart. In the rich broad valley the river winds among the poplars ; everything is flooded with the beauty that has now broken all about the world.

*In the neighbourhood of Amiens. The battalion had moved some distance to the south.

The spongecake and writing paper received with thanks. ——is on his last legs and threatens to slowly and silently vanish away.

JACK

9th May 1916

DEAR MOTHER

As George Graves says, " Happy Days." We are having a semi-rest for a little and our surroundings are ideal. Only the weather has failed us somewhat, having turned coldish with showers, as I remember often happened in May in England, persuading us that to punt on the Granta was an over-rated pastime.

This village is perfectly charming, its numerous streets curl up and down hill, intersecting continually. The cottage walls are white and clean, and there are a dozen pretty nooks and unexpected vistas. Could one rebuild ——* or ——† as they stood one would find no such variety. You see I have turned my back on the country of my apprenticeship. If you saw the difference between the two you would forgive such disloyalty. Here is the infinite variety of hill and dale (even tho' the rise is slight), the gleam of the river in the wide shallow valley, grey towers cushioned on wooded slopes (I forget the line of the Allegro that just describes it), stretches of road in avenues of tall trees, and a hundred other sights.

No more for the moment.

JACK

* Festubert.   † Givenchy.

10th May 1916

Dear Mother

So sorry no time for a letter, but there is a scheme to-morrow which requires some " uffish thought." I have been busy too during Hammill's absence on a court-marshal.

Our surroundings are perfectly lovely; the weather has warmed up again and everything is enchanting. My helmet off to la belle France.

The cottages in this village have electric light.

I hope your cold is gone.

Jack

11th May 1916

Dear Mother

Still no time, or is it inclination, to write. But one is pretty well used up by the end of the day.

Tactical exercises to-day, in which I was strafed by the C.O. for not having seen and reported on some troops in the background. The mid-day meal reclining on the pleasant downs among the white-thorn. Afterwards Company operations, B Company in co-operation with A practising the advance through a wood. This was most amusing. The woods rang with shouts, queries, and expostulations. Harvey marched his platoon on a compass bearing which took him careering right across the front of several others, to their bewilderment and indignation. We emerged at last.

Then there was a race home for the officers, to the cheers of the soldiery. I got in third, not ill-pleased with myself at leaving the athletes behind, most of them falling out. —— the wiry backwoodsman was first and won the 100 francs.

JACK

12th May 1916
DEAR MOTHER

As I said before there isn't enough left of us to write letters at the end of the day.

The subalterns and N.C.O.'s are now drilled together in the evenings, which is amusing and irksome at once.

The blossom is thick in the orchards and the trees are daily deeper cushioned in the rich grass.

We bathed this afternoon in the river ——*. The C.O. has put me down for yet another job, having strafed me only the other morning for failing to do it. But my coming in third in the race restored me to favour.

JACK

14th May
DEAR MOTHER

I am afraid my letters will get duller and duller, as the censorship is strong on the wing just now, and I am rather conscience stricken for former indiscretions. I am only glad that I got that important piece of information through before the strings tightened.

* Somme.

The weather has rather broken, and I was not for bathing yesterday in the windswept pools of the valley marshes. To-day we have taken upon ourselves to be At Home, and give a gymkhana performed by the officers. A band will play—the scene is an ancient camp on the downs behind—and all the company mess-kits are being borrowed to provide tea. It will probably be amusing, tho' I confess I don't like being roped in for athletic or any other contests on the one day when I hoped to have some freedom. I have decided though that it is anti-social to protest.

—— made a slight splash this week. Hearing of the officers' drill class under the S.M., he wrote to the Adjutant announcing his inability to join in on the score of age (he is thirty-eight). This was ignored and he sat down to write his resignation—we always have to help him to compose these things. I don't know what became of this last, but the C.O. ordered Hammill to bring him to a better frame of mind.

Did I tell you that Vaudrey had got a delightful job, instructing officers somewhere behind —— ? Our separation is my main regret at our change, coming as it did just when he was perfectly accessible.

JACK

15th May 1916

DEAR MOTHER

The cake and handkerchief with thanks.

I have just got a new job* (unless I am shortly found unsuitable and fired out incontinent); it almost seems to be the goods at last. It is a Brigade affair and

* Command of Brigade Scouts.

I shall be pretty well on my own, with a band of myrmidons whose training I am to take in hand to-morrow. I shall have to keep the Brigadier informed, during the operations which are presumably the consummation of the present phase, of the movements and whereabouts of the wandering units of his command. So you see it is quite cushy and safe. I never expected the C.O. to recommend me to the Brigade just after strafing me the other morning; and some of the Battalion Scout Officers I met this morning at our conference are far more efficient. It remains for me to strengthen my present precarious foothold.

I was asked to Brigade Head-Quarters at tea-time to-day to discuss the affair. The place is a chateau with an alluring name, and is a graceful house standing in beautiful grounds, though the garden has rather run to seed; but its trees are still delightful, screening the grounds from the river except for a pretty glimpse. Inside are stately rooms carved walls and ceilings and a rearguard of expensive furniture. The Brigade Major was very agreeable. Of the General it must be confessed that, except perhaps to a chosen circle, he has little social appeal.

The gymkhana yesterday was acclaimed a vast success. The surroundings were almost phenomenal, a spacious valley along the Roman camp with terraces formed by nature or man. The best show was the "Balaclava Melee," in which two teams of officers bareback on mules tried to beat cockades out of opponents' steel helmets with clubs of bound straw.

Please discontinue the *Bystander*—this no doubt to your relief; we have a surfeit of it.

JACK

16th May 1916

DEAR MOTHER

To-day was my first day with my new command. The C.O. pokes fun at me for deserting the regiment, as practically I have done. He didn't anticipate how detached I was to be. However he lends telescopes and field glasses with a lavish hand. Such jolly country.* I would send my humble sketches but fear the censor.

I had quite fun with my motley band gathered from the four corners of the Brigade, and made them do a number of things.

I do hope you will enjoy your trip, tho' where is Kettlewell?

I have had a charming letter from Mr. Radclyffe. He and his boys went down to Devonshire to look for work. They sowed vegetables and later found jobs on a poultry farm.

It is a beauteous evening, bats and cock-chafers fill the air. This kitchen garden and the cottage roofs beyond it are worlds removed from any firing line.

JACK

18th May 1916

DEAR MOTHER

I am cut to the heart at missing writing yesterday, but trust this will get off, though that is slightly problematic.

* They had by now moved further south, into the Amiens district.

I am moved to Brigade H.Q. for a few days at any rate, while the Battalion is away. I shall have my hands full to-morrow training Scouts and cleaning billets at the same time. These are strenuous days for me, but not without their reward; or so I thought to-day, as I saw coherence and clearness taking shape in the messages my brood are set to write. The day's work is not ended of course with the roaming about, as one has to make arrangements for the next day.

My understudy is a pleasant if rather fish-like creature, his accent not above reproach. I slept in the garden last night and was much bitten by mosquitoes.

In haste
JACK

21st May 1916

DEAR MOTHER

These are strange days. The village streets are so quiet, with the regiment that peopled them gone. I remain as sole representative, living in state at Brigade H.Q. with a mixed train of men under my charge, a few crocks, some carpenters who may be called for any moment, stragglers who return from hospital and are attracted to this rearguard by gravitation, and a chorus of Scouts of first and second magnitude, some of them mine, the others Hornby's. The chief trouble is that we were only told to dump the carpenters at the last moment, and consequently there are no rations drawn for them here. The Brigade Q.M.Sgt. has helped me nobly, but I have continually to dive into shops after stores to keep the wolf from the door.

Meanwhile I carry on with my Scouts, who are learning a few things. I am also responsible for the Battalion Scouts, but now they have given me another officer, one Pedder, a most charming fellow who has been attached to the Brigade Staff for some time.

But the days are really strange, and more so than any period of my adventures so far, because of what they are and what they might be. For we live in this beautiful house surrounded by beauty and the hundred graces of dignified and spacious living; the tall windows open on the garden (where the grass has run riot) with its screen of splendid beeches and chestnuts; behind them is the river, which is every day more lovely and peaceful in this radiant May weather; the Corot landscape on the further side a dream of beauty. Our cool bathes are the doings of peace, and old furniture and curtains about the house remind one of other days. On an afternoon you may see the gleam of a tablecloth down on the lawn with garden chairs about it, and at night from the the dining room windows the great trees are sombre and lowering silhouettes against their dark starry back-ground, like a Dulac picture in a Christmas book.

And of course it is all merely setting, marred at every turn by discordant notes.

We are a mixed assemblage of an evening. At the head is the General, a thin white-haired old man with a head rather too large, suggesting the big-headed trout one sees. He has very little social charm, though his smile when he looks up is quite appealing; he is often silent for a long time, when the conversation of the others gives the effect that he isn't there, or if present is better ignored. Next comes the Brigade-Major, a young Regular recently from Gallipoli. I don't suppose he has any remarkable gifts but he is a quite unusually nice person. Possibly he isn't so young, but he has the smoothest and freshest face you ever saw. He generally leads the conversation with attacks on Pedder. There is a pretty violent swing of the pendulum and we come to Vellacott, who is at present answering for Sewell. He attacks all and sundry with Sayre's co-operation. Next him is the Interpreter, a tall Frenchman with a figure like Mr. Radclyffe, and a freckly face rather like a camel's. He talks English distinctly well and is a very agreeable companion. An entirely different element is supplied by his left-hand neighbour, Micheson the Signalling Officer. He is also tall and thin as a lath, though more graceful than the Interpreter. He would probably have stayed up at Oxford and become a Don, if not for the war. As it is he is a most efficient O.C. Signals, I believe. He talks in a very cultured manner, and is most manierè, standing in stained glass attitudes and emphasizing his conversation by means of his large eyes. He has a scar on his face, a souvenir I believe of the first phase of the war, in which he played some humbler part. On the other side of me is Pedder, who has an innocent and angelic expression (which after all he lives up to), and is otherwise entirely normal. Last is the Vet. who is comparatively burly, and beyond a slightly pensive expression calls for no comment.

I may be here some time. Will you address my letters 56th Inf. Bde. H.Q.?

JACK

23rd May 1916

DEAR MOTHER

I was delighted to get my post to-day —the first that has reached me since my move here.

I am so glad to think of your holiday in Yorkshire. It must have been a perfect oasis.

The mingled woe and pleasure I think I explained later—that it meant going right away from any chance of seeing Vaudrey, on which I had counted now that he is stationary in a School of Instruction. There is too a touch of regret for even the scattered stones of that desolate country, and for places where we drew our first memorable impressions of the war. They were not unhappy days.

On the other hand, who would not rejoice at this different country-side, the sweeping downs and climbing woods and exquisite glades, nightingale haunted ? The Interpreter was saying last night he wished we could all see as much of France as the variations of the battle-line afford the sight of.

The General was in good form to-night and quoted amusing rhymes. Micheson too is in great form in these days, with his element of what one might call cultured humour. We have been joined by Surridge of Cambridge, the Bombing Officer, returned from measles.

I was so sorry to hear of Mrs. James Taylor's son. Will you tell her when you see her.

I don't know what's become of the regiment. They will possibly re-appear among the Russians on the Eastern front.

Some Muscatol would be acceptable. The mosquitoes are frightful.

JACK

P.S. The General uses it.

24th May 1916

DEAR MOTHER

This evening witnesses my most comic downfall. Since Surridge's return the position at Brigade H.Q. has been rather absurd, it being quite irregular to have so many officers about. So I really had to go. Picture me then dining in a cottage with the Trench Mortars, who have a very dirty table-cloth, and sleeping in a cubby hole of a room next door to my motley troop. The company is far less distinguished, all Second Lieutenants. They include an Irishman of frankly disloyal sentiments. A further touch is our new Transport Officer, just turned up. Meeting him in the road I took him for a bandmaster or something similar. He is a bald and almost tottering old gentleman with a monocle, having three sons in the war. I can't picture him strafing the transport.

Going through a village to-day whom should I meet but Sanderson of Donkin's. We were in the 5th together and got on very well. I had expected to meet him at dinner at H.Q. to-night, but on my return from scouting found my orders, and as he appeared in slacks on the chateau drive I was just scurrying away like a fallen angel to my cottage in the vale.

We had our first rain to-day for weeks. There was also a roll of thunder but the spectacular affair I expected never came off.

JACK

28th May 1916

Dear Mother

To-day the village streets will fill again. I shall be glad to see them all. Tho' I fear we are losing Ridley; it was inevitable; I hear he is to be a Staff Captain.

On the whole I shan't be sorry to lose my motley gang of Battalion Scouts, sick men, returners from leave, &c. My own Scouts I have now brought down to a roomy billet near by, and they seem to be settling in very comfortably.

I was rather naughty last night at supper, and quite infuriated the aged Transport Officer by my remarks in a political discussion; but he was so outrageously overbearing and bigoted that I couldn't help it, though I promise you I said nothing but what was right and proper. He is quite mollified this morning. I was rather sorry tho', because it is so sporting of him to have come out here at all. I hope the C.O., who leads Transport Officers rather a dance, will be kind to him.

Voelcker Pedder and I had a charming tea together yesterday afternoon in the chateau garden. Afterwards we tried to navigate Pedder's preposterous punt, a sort of box knocked up for him by someone in the A.S.C. Pedder is almost as pastoral as Ridley.

As for my job, I am called Brigade Scout Officer, and exist to keep " the old min " in touch with the progress of his command during an action. I believe the General takes very little interest in the business, but the Brigade Major (Vellacott at present, Sayres normally) is splendid and helps a lot. I doubt if the General knew why I was at Brigade Head-Quarters at all. He treated me at once with courtesy and vagueness.

Please thank Father for the Clemak blades. I am so glad you have summer at last.

The personage who saw our manœuvres the other day made no observation.

JACK

29th May 1916

DEAR MOTHER

Amusing days for me, especially yesterday which I enjoyed vastly. For one thing I like the later rising and the comparative freedom from Scouts. Then the regiment was due to return early in the afternoon, and I was up and down the village ordering lunches for returning officers and chatting with the folk. Many of them were delighted at the prospect, and I had a pleasant half-hour in A Company's mess, where I was given some capital cider, and we drank the healths of the aged parents who had come in from a neighbouring village. The folk were a cut above the peasant class and were enthusiastic in praise of Hewlett and his brood, whose names they knew and pronounced very oddly. After lunch I dispatched my rabble to their Company billets, and presently the Battalion arrived, very dusty and hot, preceded by a posse of broken men who had been sent on from the last halt in case they should drop behind and be no more seen. They were only held together by Bell, whom I found in rear, perspiring but cheerful, having urged them on all the way by spirited whistling of their favourite airs. The C.O. received me rather stuffily, for reasons which I will explain. He said something about a Course, which was bewildering, as I had just been told I was going up to the line on Wednesday to have a look round. To go on a six weeks Course would be throwing one's hand in just when I had brought my Scouts down to H.Q. Surridge, the Brigade Bombing Officer, and late of Downing I believe, had asked me to dinner at Brigade H.Q. I went to the office first to enquire about my movements, and had to run the gauntlet on the drive of the General the C.O. and Sewell. The C.O. was clearly in no over affable mood and the subjects were Vellacott and self. Vellacott is now answering for Sayres and lingers on with the Brigade, so that we have standing jokes about his answering next for the Vet. Officer and the Interpreter; but the C.O., who has lost his adjutant, is furious. Similarly he wasn't told that I, in capacity of Scout Officer, would leave him, and is most indignant. Vellacott and I stood about in the office trying not to be seen through the French windows, and waiting for the colloquy on the drive to end. The General slashed at pebbles with his cane. Surridge and Pedder were frankly frivolous and irresponsible. We slipped eventually by a back way into the dining-room, where we were joined by Micheson the Interpreter and the Vet., and behaved in a foolish and pre-war manner and made very merry. The General was very late but showed no signs of storm and stress, and we had a most pleasant evening. I was quite glad to be there again. The General had confused me with Captain Hoyle of the other regiment and thought I had been attached to H.Q. for some transport stunt; he had been much suprised at my departure. He was in great form last night, and revealed himself as a very charming and cultured old gentleman. In point of fact he likes to be thought rather a gay old dog, with a risqué French flavour.

Any way I am to go on a Course on Thursday, lasting about five weeks. The C.O. has other designs for me than my present occupation, which looks as if it would go by the board as far as I am concerned. Indeed I shall have to return my Scouts, with thanks, to their battalions.

I am perfectly delighted to hear about your pleasant picnics and excursions, which according to Margaret seem to have brought practically unclouded pleasure.

Besides the Rgt. please address me : School of Instruction, H.Q. 19th Division, B.E.F.

JACK

2nd June 1916

DEAR MOTHER

Here I am installed in another chateau, grander, but newer and less beautiful then the last.* We all drifted in here yesterday afternoon. When I rode up I found the verandah filled with faces rather bootlike, such expression as they wore suggesting boredom and a sort of despair, as if all arrangements were awry. To my no small disgust I found that I was senior, and as such would have to run the mess, which starts from practically nothing at all except the plate knife &c.

*At Domart

that officers bring with them. As I had come here with very special purposes I was much bored at the prospect of devoting time and thought to such things. However I trust that all may yet be well.

Except for that fly the prospect is cheering. The Commandant is a charming man. I dined with him last night; over the soup we found that he is a cousin of Mrs. Easebourne Hoyle. One side of the dining room consists almost entirely of French windows, so that you seem to be nearly in the garden.

No time for more just now.

JACK

3rd June 1916

DEAR MOTHER

Just a line. As I have decided not to care tuppence about the mess, as long as it's not too appalling and I don't get lynched, I am feeling much better. Because really it would be absurd if, having coming here to learn things, I were continually distracted by problems of serving tables, simply through the accident of seniority.

The garden is finer than the house. The place stands on a plateau, and through the house is screened by beeches and thick copses, the designer, for it must be designed tho' most skilfully contrived, has left open vistas, and from windows you see over the plateau's verge the blues and greens that cloud and sun make on the lower distance.

No time for more just now.

JACK

5th June 1916

DEAR MOTHER

Things were clouded for us on Saturday afternoon by the news from Jutland, tho' we felt that it was no moral defeat. Since then further German losses are reported. But it is terrible to think of the loss of life. I feel too very much for Teddy who will surely feel it keenly.

I made a long and pleasant expedition yesterday, our free day, breakfasting on the road off excellent omelettes in a pub, and reading Euripides' Alcestis (in the original which I find I remember very well except the grammar) with the greatest pleasure. I reached and explored a town some twelve miles off and returned by train. On getting in about half-past six, Lane, who acts as a sort of adjutant here, told me I was to dine with the Major on the strength of an announcement in the paper, which you will have seen.* It fair took my breff away and it was some minutes before I was quite sure they were not pulling my leg. One ———, a quaint creature with a slow heavy manner, had got it too and the Major was delighted. When we went in he wrung our hands and drank our health. It was odd this morning having my hand seized at breakfast by someone whose name I didn't know and whom I had thought rather unattractive. We had rather an ordeal this morning. Major Molloy came on parade when Lane was drilling us with the N.C.O.'s and called out ——— and me and a Sergeant; to drill them I thought. We had to march out (we were carrying our servants' rifles) and stand facing the throng. The Major then made a speech

* His Military Cross

about us and shook our disengaged hands, after which we returned to our places. Looking at the paper later I was delighted to see that Payton Hadley had got it, and also Hornby, who is perfectly fearless. For myself I wish that Harvey could have recognition; he was left alone that night with his awful device in front of the wire, the whole venture still before him full of the risks and horrors of scrapping, while I crawled cushily back.

———— was full of exploits when the regiment went up the line. He was under arrest most of the time, for bombing fish in water near the town; but when free he stood on the parapet in broad daylight and fired at hares between the lines; and when that was unsuccessful, at a horse and cart that appeared behind the German trenches. Eventually a shrapnel was sent over which knocked him almost senseless.

Enough for the present.

JACK

8th June 1916

DEAR MOTHER

I never seem to write to you now-a-days.

We are settling down to the Course and I for one am learning quite a lot. The Course is one of general instruction and has no particular reference to Machine Guns, nor am I to deal with those infernal engines. It is indeed another Camberley (what a time that was), except that there a lot was done for us that we have to do for ourselves here, and also that at the Staff College the bath question had been considered and dealt with in most excellent fashion, while here—well this is France, a country apparently of non-bathers. If you saw the room where Colville the R.E. man and I sleep you would be delighted. It is a large room quite grandly furnished, with chairs and tables all about, and one wakes to beautiful views down the vistas of the trees. The garden is fascinating, the path that skirts the fringe crosses the open rides and plunges into black tunnels of delicate trees that seem trained to make the arch. Alluring by-paths lead away into the depths, and the garden straggles off into deep woods where you can have enchanting walks.

There are a lot of partridges about and I think the place is a shooting box. The man has another house in Paris; a peacock yells in his stableyard; in another outbuilding this afternoon we found his dog-cart, his phaeton and his motor car; he himself they tell us is a private soldier. We thought of him this afternoon in the falling rain.

I don't know yet whether at the end of the month I shall see my Scouts again, or whether they will lie low with their Battalions until they are wanted for the real goods, or whether I've done with them for ever. The C.O. wants me to command one of the Companies on my return.

I knew nothing about the Military Cross; it was an entire surprise on Sunday. Many thanks for all your letters, including Margaret's which came to-day. Its chief point for me is the pleasure it brings all of you at home; for myself I can only say that countless others have done so much more, unrewarded, and that I could wish the others, especially Harvey, had recognition.

Will you thank Father for the Muscatol and mosquito net; the weather has been unsuitable for a trial of the latter.

JACK

10*th June* 1916

DEAR MOTHER

Many thanks for your letter. I received to-day a charming letter from Madeleine Fox about the iron cross.

Which Mr. Sutton did Margaret hear from? Was it the great and inevitable Sutton of Rugby and Pembroke?

Hopkins is a charming youth, you would like him very much. He is very young and has a queer sheepish expression. But his leave must be nearly up. You never saw a happier sight than him and Pringle on a glorious summer morning boarding the mess-cart, to drive to a neighbouring railway station.

I am getting to like the fraternity here much better. One fellow, in the Machine Gun Corps, whom I thought quite objectionable at first, proves far better and we get on quite well. He is an actor, having toured with Martin Harvey, whom he worships, in "The Only Way," and later appearing in music halls in piano stunts. At his instigation I have advertised a concert and arranged to borrow a piano from the Wireless, but it looks as if it will be a benefit for Grove, on the Actors' Benevolent principle, helped out with sentimentals from the N.C.O.'s.

Most people are desolate to-night as ———* has been put out of bounds, and it's a Saturday night.

We spend the day out, pencils (several), map, sketching-block, and india-rubber in hand, armed also with compass and field glasses, and our N.C.O.'s in tow, working out defence schemes and what not. At other times we drill, and are learning all manner of smart tips which I shall impart to the Regiment with some gusto when I return. We are drilled by a Lieutenant in the ——— who is a sort of Adjutant here. At first I rather disliked a heavy heartiness in his manner to the Commandant; until he drilled us and then it was as clear as daylight; of course he was an ex-Sergeant in the Guards. To hear him gives one an impression of Aldershot in—say 1913.

JACK

11th June 1916

DEAR MOTHER

I hope you are enjoying your holiday in London. I can't think of any plays you would like, as there is so much of the George Robey business about now. "Disraeli" perhaps and "Daddy-Long-Legs."

I have just told my servant (a ridiculous but very faithful old man) to sew a length of white and purple ribbon on my coat. ——— and I have been ordered to put it up.

The regiment has moved lately to a village nearer here and I went yesterday evening to cadge supper from B. Company. They live in rather a dilapidated place, but

* Amiens.

with quite an attractive orchard in which some of them have tents. These villages are rather odd. On a first glance a whole street seems falling to pieces, but looking through a gap in peeling walls you will see a trim path leading up through flowering beds to a neat and charming house.

I was waiting for Colvill in a village square this morning, watching them tugging at the bell-ropes in the church porch. Then came the clanging of a hand-bell in the offing, and a mild but rather excited-looking old man appeared with a paper. He planted himself in the sleepy square and began to read out his proclamation. It was an amusing scene. Two men in Sunday best who were standing by the Church drew a few steps nearer ; a woman appeared in a barn doorway ; a labourer going into his cottage stopped and looked over his shoulder. The reader seemed pleased on the whole with this audience and carried on. But it was rather an empty house. His notice was a warning that bombing practice would be carried out to-morrow in a field near by—not, as I had expected, some dramatic announcement about the war.

JACK

13th June 1916

DEAR MOTHER

I'm so glad you saw Hopkins. He was bound to prove satisfactory.

It is turning out a disgusting June, wet and cold to a degree. There was a violent hailstorm to-day to add to the other showers, and we, engaged on an outpost scheme, were soaked.

I have had a charming note from Mr. Fox. I do think it was good of him to write. Betty sent me a long letter, and Auntie Mabel and Uncle James have of course been splendid. Salter writes from Grantham, where he is Adjutant to a Machine Gun Company, " Morris dancing vindicated, Swanwick justified."

I looked in at C. Company the other evening. Lumley did a wild dance and introduced me as a prodigy to the daughter of the house; Bell was perfectly charming and crowed with unaffected delight.

Really I am rather an impostor; it was because the limelight was on the show that I got anything out of it. By the way, the Sergeant who stood up in front of the Germans and swore and expostulated has got the D.C.M.

As for what you ask at the end of your London letter, although it will be my season due, I very much doubt it.

JACK.

15th June 1916

DEAR MOTHER

I'm so glad we've re-established communication again.

Of course I ought to have acknowledged your telegram. I got it on Monday morning. Herewith Joe's and Mrs. Hadley's letters, which I was delighted to get.

We are threatened with having to turn out of here and live where, as Gilbert Murray translates, "the little things of the woodland move unseen." We were dismayed of course, but it looks as if it would blow over. After such comfort "it would be a dismal thing to do." You see what pampered Chocolate Soldiers we are now. For once it hasn't rained, and we were able to make sketches &c. without deluging showers. I received a pat on the back the other evening from the chief of the Divisional Staff, or G.S.O.1, who hailed me as I crossed the lawn. He comes over occasionally to give lectures. He is a curious man, an absolute farceur in a way. Sewell always makes out that he is a sort of maitre de ballet at D.H.Q. My first encounter with him was on the morning after our stunt, when he came to Battalion H.Q. to hear about it. That was a weird interview. We three just roused from our belated rest, with the mud still on our uniforms, (Coxen's wash has been of the sketchiest) sat round a sort of drain pipe they had at H.Q. there, with the C.O. as impressario, Sewell to represent the Battalion and looking meek for once, and the G.S.O.1 as interested enquirer. His manner was that of a light comedy vicar rather than a soldier; he has an odd way of inclining his head and blinking his eyes, and on this occasion there was a great deal of "quite so" and "exactly" &c., in fact he was a perfect Follies' parson. His bland attitude struck our rather tumultuous feelings as the very quintessence of the Staff as represented by their detractors. When he lectured too here, he did one or two pieces of intentional buffoonery. I'm afraid this is a very unattractive portrait and you mustn't think that he is not a good and capable man, which from all accounts he is.

I have ceased to bother about the mess. We have a capital cook and a capable corporal, also the officers' caterer is splendid. We have periodical mess meetings which are quite amusing ; there was some excitement last night.

It's sad to see what havoc I have caused among the wounded at Bakewell.

Ypres and Verdun are terrible as you say. I think Ypres is the worst, because there is a certain glamour and a far more obvious raison d'être in Verdun, while Ypres is merely a side show. It is amazing to think what a cushy time our own lot have had in this war.

JACK

16th June 1916

DEAR MOTHER

There was some excitement here yesterday, when the unusual sound of carriage wheels was heard on the drive, and a fly drove up containing none other than Monseigneur himself, accompanied by his mother. A train of house-keepers and maid-servants, who live mysteriously in the attics, descended the stairs, and, after what appeared a but tepid encounter and not the feudal demonstration I had hoped for, the boxes were taken upstairs (a quite homely scene recalling the labours of Joe and Worsencroft when anybody arrives) and the lord of the manor spirited away, almost smuggled, in the same direction with his mother, a rather undistinguished old lady whom I haven't set eyes on since she passed through this morning on her way to the little church at the front gate, in very rustling black.

A few days ago I described the master of the house as a toiling poilu, ordered about possibly by his tailor in a Sam Browne. Now at any rate he is a Lieutenant, and in the Ordnance at that, so he isn't so much to be pitied. Apparently tho' he was wounded, and he is now having sick leave.

Imagine returning from the ward to a stately 'ome crowded with English subalterns, who have made the front hall their mess and occupy the chief bedrooms. We heard the Major explaining matters to him on the landing.

But he took it extraordinarily calmly, and when some of us later returned from our after-dinner stroll we found him on the drive talking with others. So we had a pleasant chat, he behaving as if he was our guest. He talks a little English and, with both languages shockingly pronounced by the opposing sides, we got on famously and compared notes about the various places we knew in England, where he apparently had made a tour of the cathedral towns. Then we parted with courteous ceremony, he saluting. Later however on his way upstairs he found us in the mess, and we celebrated him in Benedictine and had further conversation, chiefly about the sports of the two countries. We learned too that French and German patrols had scrapped just up the road. Then a repetition of the good-night ceremonial and the interview closed. I believe he has his meals in the attic. Our staff still carry on in the dining-room with the windows that make you feel you are in the garden. Was there ever such a thing?

To-day it has been summer again. On my way out this morning to our theatre of operations I found two R.E. Officers with a punctured side-car. One of them proved to be the great Jasper Holmes, the Muscular Christian, pillar of religious society in Cambridge and ring-leader at Swanwick. The blue-eyed Thompson was his devoted follower. I learnt that the latter has now chucked his hand in about the war and gone off to enunciate philosophy in Madras.

The last time I met Jasper was at a place in Westminster on our way to the U.P.S. at Epsom. He was in a most bloodthirsty mood, and I remember thinking that the surplice had slipped pretty effectively and revealed the mailed shirt.

I wish now I had made Armitage go and see you when you were in London.
JACK

17th June 1916
DEAR FATHER

Very many thanks for letters and parcels of the last few days. And in anticipation for those coming. The tobacco I received to-night.

I fear I can't be induced to apply for leave. It is an unwise thing to do.

I was more than pleased to read yesterday that Harvey is after all mentioned in dispatches for his work that night, as also, which is excellent, L.-Cpl. Bowman, my body guard. I couldn't have wished a better one.

How very nice of the wounded men at the Hospital.
JACK

18th June 1916

DEAR MOTHER

A thunderstorm has broken out in the chateau and is only dying down now. It appears that the lord of the manor, while the British colony were having dinner, went round inspecting the rooms. In one, where six officers sleep and which we call the warren, he found some of his Louis Quinze chairs damaged. Straightway a frantic outburst and denunciations of the English. Mobilization of the household and the officers' leaders. The Major, who is a man of culture and scrupulously careful of billets he is responsible for, protests that his lot can't have done it. The officers concerned declare the damage was done before. Colvill, who is an independent witness and saw the rooms before we took over, vows that that is true. Monsieur, roused to fury, swears that the Germans couldn't have done worse and assesses the damage at 2,000 francs. Chorus of women-folk from the attics in an agitated flutter. The Major, taking the housemaid as an ally, appeals to her to support the statement that the furniture was damaged before. The hapless housemaid, all of a twitter before her enraged lord, who will round upon her, if she supports us, for not mentioning the damage at the time, declares that we must have done it. So the situation is lost and only persuasive argument can help matters now. The Interpreter arrives to-morrow morning, and Monsieur departs at noon, so we shan't have to face his scowls much longer. His mother is broken hearted at the damage but bears no malice. It is very bad luck on the Major, who is particular to fanaticism in these matters He says he will fight the business to the King before these officers are made to pay a sou.

The C.O. too of the Regt. who were here before us was most particular, so it must have been done by other various troops who have occupied this place during these eighteen months.

I had been out all afternoon, and only came in when Monsieur had withdrawn with his thunderbolts. I found the folk of the warren standing nonplussed in the Mess, and Grove the actor announced that they were all under arrest.

I had gone to the only available town in the neighbourhood to get my hair cut, which was a long-felt want. It is some thirteen miles off, but I didn't propose walking all the way this time. I had eventually to go rather further than I expected before a man turned up with an aircraft lorry. This took me a few miles and I had another walk which looked like being a long one, had not a boy driving a trap insisted on asking where I was bound for. On hearing, he and his companion, a cheerful looking man, were delighted, and deciding they were not spies in search of information from kidnapped English officers, I joined them on the crowded seat. At the top of the last hill they insisted that we should get out and have a drink at the pub. which I gathered that they had been doing all along the route, tho' none the worse for wear except that they would be very late for their meal at the man's sister's. To this repast they invited me; with some lingering suspicion perhaps of the kidnapping I refused, and repented it very much afterwards. We drank some vague white wine however and drove on, chatting pleasantly. They drove me up to a barber's in the town and there we parted on the best of terms.

I got some tea in the amusing café that opens full on the street in the continental way, and returned as before by train, with a young officer going on leave after appalling experiences in recent celebrated fighting. We compared notes. We were joined later by a handsome airman with a languid voice, who was going to Farnborough, of all places, to collect a machine in which he intends to fly back to-morrow.

The country looked too beautiful for words. It gives me absolute joy.

JACK

19th June 1916

DEAR MOTHER

Isn't it splendid that the C.O. and Harvey and little Lance-Corporal Bowman, who accompanied me, are mentioned in despatches? I should have felt quite badly if I had been the only one to make material profit out of that affair. I am particularly glad perhaps about the C.O. If there was ever a conscientious and knowledgeable Colonel he is the man.

You can imagine my pleasure too at seeing Bliss's name.

The Divisional Interpreter came along this morning. He declared that the Empire chairs (I was wrong, not Louis XV., those are in the Major's room) were 1820 at earliest, put them at £3 a piece at most, and supported us generally.

We had a concert on Saturday evening. A first rate piano was borrowed from some troops opposite and placed on the verandah where the officers sat like the

Pharisees, conspicuously facing the N.C.O's who perched on the lawn. Some of them sang very well, and one of our orderlies did " Take a pair of sparkling eyes" in as finished a way as I have ever heard. The star performer of course was Grove the actor, who can imitate to the life any comedian and most actors you choose to name, with masterly accompaniments, and is a complete entertainment in himself. These reminders of the London amusements somehow typify Blighty for us more than anything.

JACK.

I am so glad to hear from kind and faithful Mr. Dunn that you have been at Harmer Green.

21st June 1916

DEAR FATHER

Almost invariably letters from home reach me three days after the date at their head; for instance yours of the 18th has come to-day, the 21st.

My letter of the 14th was probably written on the evening of that day and would not go till the next morning. As for D.H.Q., well that is one of the things the Censor would object to my explaining. The letter of the 13th I probably forgot to put in the box.

The Nurse's book is splendid, tho' I have had very little time to read it lately. Very many thanks.

Mark's parcels (three) arrived last night, and I have been decking the mess-table with unaccustomed delights in judicious instalments of " sweetness long drawn out."

The chocolate biscuits are capital, the ginger of course one of my chief delights, the crystallised fruits always most acceptable, as also the creme-de-menthe, which went down last night like wildfire, accompanied by the preserved plums. The brawn was devoured at lunch, and the pork-pie which I put on then (the tin arrived rather bashed in, but without evil effect) greatly remarked; the herrings will appear at breakfast to-morrow; the steak-puddings are yet to come, but from what I remember of similar goods of Harvey's they aren't so successful as some of the other things. I will let you know how they go. On the whole I think the ginger and chocolate biscuits are the most useful.

The *Observer* and *New Statesman* arrived this evening.

The other night about 11 o'clock Colville and I were considering from our respective beds how on earth we could get to sleep; we had been in bed about an hour with no result. Suddenly the door opened and Grove the actor appeared in pyjamas, with an alarm of fire which he couldn't locate. But indeed, as we scrambled into some clothes, we became aware that smoke was coming into the room, and there was a very suspicious, in fact unmistakable, smell. We heard Grove, in great form, call out " Major" as he knocked at the Commandant's door. The latter is very deaf, and we heard Grove go in and shout " Fire" into his ear before there was any response. Orders are that everybody falls in on the lawn on such occasions, and it would be my job to detail a water-party. As I came on to the landing two valises completely packed and strapped up came hurtling downstairs from the second floor, one of the owners, a Machine Gunner, following, dressed for the road, spurs and all. Smoke was rising fairly thick from somewhere downstairs. Somewhere on the second floor, an officer in broken French was battering at the doors of the women's quarters. Everybody was tumbling out in various rigs, one in an Engadine cap. The least attractive member of the class was all of a twitter, declaring that the boarding on the top floor was burning hot. Down crashed the two valises on to the ground floor where we all foregathered. Then a cry came from Lane below that all was over. The scene in the hall was most comic. By now everybody, as the alarm was laid, had forgotten the fire; but they were consumed, and the house re-echoed, with Homeric laughter. We were an absurd sight at the foot of the stairs—people in every kit, headed by Durrant in his belt and spurs, grouped round the valises; in the centre was the Major in shirt and pants. To crown all the women folk now descended lights in hand. Though we reassured them, they didn't conceal their distrust of us and made straight for the basement, followed by entreaties and cries of " Fini." I followed the Major down, and we found in a cellar a forlorn litter of paper and bottle-straws soused in water. The scene down there was most striking. It came straight out of Hogarth's illustrations to Don Quixote, that I recollect in a passage at Bassfield. In the cellar, stalking about over the garbage, was the housekeeper, candle in hand; the light threw weird shadows on the stone walls and over her person and disordered dress. All the time she declaimed and soliloquised; a sort of Hecuba. Protesting and entreating and *sotto voce* swearing, stood the Major in thin khaki shirt and short aertex pants. The burden of his song was that she was a ridiculous old woman and high time she returned to bed; of hers that Monsieur when he departed that morning had commissioned her in his last words not to let his chateau be burned down, and now the dreaded thing had happened, and with such people in the house one might have known all along that it would. Ignoring the Major's chidings she rummaged in the straw and up and down the place, assisted by a disgruntled female companion, and as far as I remember we left her at it.

After that Colvill and I got to sleep.

It transpired that there had been "wretched doings" that night among some of the servants, in the course of which matches were dropped before they retired.

Great news from the Russian front. Things seem to be going pretty well generally. Did you read the Kaiser's address to Hindenberg, about German faces smiling and eyes flashing at his name?

Could I have a pair of the baggy breeches à la Guards like the ones I had last year? They are much more suitable for summer than Bedford cord.

JACK.

23rd June 1916

DEAR FATHER

The boots to my no small relief arrived yesterday and, tho' they haven't had much chance of showing their quality yet, they appear to fit perfectly.— For which thanks be.

We have just come back from a scenario at D.H.Q. where we were presented with decorations by the Major General as the Army Commander couldn't turn up. (As it was not an Investiture that ceremony might conceivably come off in England, but certainly not for some time yet.) Mother will probably like to hear all about it, and I will describe proceedings later.

I have now got another job,* extremely exalted, and feel more of a fraud every hour. I leave here to-morrow. Could I have another pair of glasses, as the strain of service has told on my present ones, and it seems that I shall want them urgently. I have to report to the Division the day after to-morrow, and that will perhaps be my address for a bit. But carry on with Rgt., not the School, in the absence of further information.

In haste.

JACK

23rd June 1916

DEAR MOTHER

I hope you left a note for Mr. Radclyffe. It was too bad he wasn't in.

No, I see no chance of getting home for an Investiture yet awhile. The presentation took place to-day. You are sure to want to hear all about it, so I will try to describe it in detail.

Cooke and I and Sgt. ——— and one of the officer's servants were summoned during the drill hour this morning. Off came our ribbons, and steel helmets

---

* Divisional Forward Observing and Liaison Officer.

were provided from somewhere. We were then whisked away in one of the Divisional cars, with Major Molloy as a sort of sponsor. We expected to be late, but reached the D.H.Q. about an hour before the time. I was enthralled by the house, which was grey stone with seventeenth century decorative work all about. There was a most picturesque stable yard with a hexagonal pigeon house or something of the sort in the centre. Cooke and I lurked around, keeping out of the way of the Staff who seemed to be everywhere. Fortunately the garden gave excellent opportunities of cover. The ceremony was evidently to take place on the lawn behind the house. By now the troops who formed the chorus were beginning to arrive, and to my no small alarm I saw that the Regiment had been detailed. Next we were told to wait by a corner of the house so that we should be ready when wanted. There we sat, in a gradually increasing group, while the various troops arrived and formed up, and the Staff sauntered about arranging things. On the whole I didn't look forward to such a ceremony in front of so many people I knew. At this point the Divisional band struck up the waltz "Sizilietta," which seemed a sensationally absurd touch to an atmosphere grotesque enough already. Then we were summoned by a Staff Major and answered the roll, after which we fell in line with our backs (fortunately) to the hollow square of soldiery and facing a table and a flag pole, up which presently they began to manipulate a rather reluctant Union Jack. On my left was Hornby, frankly bored. By now the Staff had all collected under the trees that bordered the lawn facing us; the flag was in position, the last recipient of an honour had been safely gathered in (a perfectly charming Sapper, rather like Varvill, who dashed up at the last moment, having come all the way from just behind the line where he had been taking working parties), and there was an expectant stir from which emerged the Major General, a vast Homeric figure, with an A.D.C. and the A.A.Q.M.G. We had expected the Army Commander but he was unable to appear. The assembled troops did the general salute and the G.O.C. carried on. By him stood his A.D.C. with the ribbons in a document tray. The A.A. Q.M.G. had the list of names, which he called out, following with a narrative of what it was all about. I did not consider myself in the same class as the people who had done all sorts of things under heavy fire.

The Major General is perhaps not so attractive near to as he undoubtedly is a little further off; near to he looks a trifle Bacchic and burly—but imposing and distinguished nevertheless. Each recipient advanced, halted a few paces off, saluted, took a step nearer, had the thing pinned on, shook hands, saluted, about turned and rejoined the ranks. As a matter of fact there was a succession of variations on this theme. When my turn came lines and lines were read out, some of which I had certainly not done. Just as many "other ranks," you'll be glad to hear, were decorated as officers, one being an officer's servant. When the list was done the General said a few words. As the recipients were the fourth side of the square, and a barrier between him and the troops, we had to be manœuvered out of the way, which was rather amusing. The A.A.Q.M.G. conducted this move, rather uncertain as to what term to call us by. When we had been safely disposed of, we faced the crowd (my brother officers had faces like boots), and the General made one of his calm and casual speeches, intended perhaps to give the impression of a large reserve of power, which I think they do. It was rather a curious scene. On one side was the graceful house, on the other three the trees and shrubs that close in the lawn where we were grouped. There were scarlet tabs everywhere, and names had just been read out of places of mud and flatness and ruin that seemed to belong to another world. Behind us was the band ready to burst into a jaunty tune. Very faintly in the distance were the thumping vibrations of the guns.

Three cheers were given for the King; then we turned about again. The General stationed himself on our right, and we were all in line with the flag. The dusty troops marched past to a terrific noise from the band, and the whole thing was over.

But not for me—Major Molloy, before we started out, had hurriedly explained to me about some new job for which he had detailed me. During the ceremony I had been vaguely aware that the eye of Capt. Parish, the G.S.O.3, was on me. I was strolling off after the show, and having bumped into the A.A. Q.M.G., who held my arm and smiled most charmingly if abstractedly, I saw Parish approaching. He said I was to leave the School the next day and go back to the Regiment, reporting to him the day after. Then he congratulated me very nicely, and I withdrew overwhelmed. Molloy then collected his brood and we went back in the car, like successful cows returning from a show, amid the undisguised interest of the homing troops, who took us in good part considering the dust we raised.

Grove insisted that we should have the piano in again, and we had another concert. The next day I went off on his horse he kindly lent. At the entrance of the village where the Battalion lies now I met the 2nd in Command, who is always good fun. Then the C.O. turned up, followed by Hewlett, and really it was quite a home coming. The C.O. wrung my hand and said he had meant to write, and was entirely delightful altogether. So too was Vellacott, and indeed all the rest, and as I was a free lance until the morrow it was a most happy day. Hopkins I found at H.Q. doing Asst. Adjt. Of course he had simply loved seeing you and was almost speechless with admiration. He says I talk exactly like Margaret. I had a very cheery lunch at H.Q. where they carried on, or the C.O. at least, in a most ridiculous way with the two women of the place. In the afternoon I went with the Medical Officer and the R.C. padre in the mess cart to——. The padre, who is as Oirish as Somerville and Ross, was in the wildest excitement and asked us if we had "ever seen the loik now," every few minutes.

But I must close this for the present.

JACK

25 *June* 1916

28*th June* 1916

DEAR MOTHER

My present job is practically the same as the one with the Brigade in May but on a far bigger scale. It is appallingly responsible, but I rejoice at it.

I left off before, where we were setting out for ———* in the mess-cart. There were three of us on the seat, and the Padre was wild-eyed with excitement and pleasure ; the combined effect must have been good, because everyone we saw broke into smiles or laughter, and even the military police could scarce forbear to cheer.

———* has fine shops of course, and the cathedral is most impressive. Certain defensive measures take some of the effect off at present.

I went off this morning, with many farewells, to Divisional Head Quarters. This is the most elegant chateau I have seen; tho' the marble inside is imitation, its effect isn't at all bad. I found Parish's branch of the Staff in the billiard room upstairs, a place with a lovely flowery paper and opening out of an ante-room with latticed doors. We went down to the dining-room, charming in white with crimson hangings. The third of the party was ———, the Divisional M.G. Officer, a big creature with a heavy sort of face rather like a Chinaman's. There we pored over enthralling maps and photographs all the morning.

At lunch time Cox took me over to the village school, and I became a temporary member of No. 3 mess. At the head is the A.D.M.S. (Asst. Director of Medical Service) a calm and very amiable man, in face slightly recalling Bliss ; next is the A.D. Vet. S., a Major, who turned up for the first time to-day ; he was very quiet and gave a most bucolic impression. Besides these are the D.A.D.M.S., a young and tall

* Amiens.

Captain, very clever probably to have gained this position, and a person of considerable charm, full of little alert gestures ; Bertrand the Liaison Officer, who came and saved the situation for us the other day at the School of Instruction, a very nice fellow; Cox; and the anti-gas officer, a fragile looking youth.

I share a tent in the garden with Cox, tho' last night I spent out in my valise and mosquito net. I spent most of the day yesterday with the maps and photographs, tip-toeing into the billiard room to avoid collisions with the G.S.O. 1, who sat most of the day speechless and plunged in thought.

To-day Cox and I had a very curious excursion. Parish was to have come with us but couldn't. So Cox and I set off, armed with maps and telescopes, in the Daimler, to a commanding hill to watch the proceedings. I was glad to find that from my study of the photographs I picked up the villages, &c. without difficulty. There, right away before us was the War, like a print of some battle of Wellington's. We saw the shells flash and the columns of smoke rising. Villages that were already skeletons of themselves were being pounded a little further, and others, where the trees were still green, were getting a foretaste. Up hill and down dale the winding lines of chalk marked the trenches. We stayed some time identifying the places and then strolled back to the car.

A grim silence prevailed in G. office, probably because the General was there sitting in the G.S.O. 1's chair, wearing a pair of spectacles like Aunt Katie's, and looking simply portentous. All conversation was in whispers. Parish even seemed rather subdued. Indeed before we started out I slipped out of the room to avoid being present at a violent strafe that was descending on him from G.S.O. 1.

JACK

29th June 1916

DEAR MOTHER

These are thrilling days. I am frightfully pleased about the new job and very anxious not to make a mess of it.

Cox and I have moved a bit now and are at present marooned but comfortable, sojourning with the Divisional Scouts in a village of strangers. We went up to a redoubt yesterday to have a look at the line, but could not get a decent view. It was the first I had seen of trench warfare for months; as rain was falling we got a taste of the old days, and in half an hour were draggled spectacles. Our way led through a town* that is as remarkable a sight as you could wish to see. The church is gutted, though the tower, chipped in every direction, still sticks up by a miracle; it is topped by a statue, a most lovely and charming piece of work, which still hangs on, but bent right over and pointing down into the street like the tassel of a nightcap . . . . otherwise the church is no great architectural loss. It stands in the Place, which is nearly a desert with little heaps of bricks, but streets lead off every way still practically intact, with flowers in the gardens. Yet

* Albert.

they contrive to look far more dreary than the square, for the shattered windows have empty rooms behind them and almost all the houses look dead. On the pavement are bins of rubbish which look as if someone was coming to take them away. Some of the roofs have shell holes and occasionally an upper story, completely wrecked, looks as if it must fall soon. And yet down these unutterably forlorn streets you see a few civilians passing, and unexpectedly a door will open and someone appear. In a few cases shops carry on with quite a gay display, and somewhere I know there is an Officers' Tea-room of great merit.

As we passed practically in solitude up a long dreary street the precarious windows shook to the guns which are all about. Indeed I was glad of some cotton wool.

As we left our redoubt we had to run the gauntlet of the eighteen pounders which were blazing away about two hundred yards off, so that in places where the trench was low we were fanned by hot gusts—but with wool it was all right.

On reaching this village we found that the Division wasn't coming just yet—the Town Major helped us to billets. We found him having tea on a sort of dais in a room crowded with Doctors playing bridge. Their Colonel insisted on us having tea before anything else was done. After a rather boring day this was welcome.

We are installed in a house that the Major-General will shortly occupy. The old couple are refugees— the woman is of quite preposterous dimensions and practically shapeless. Her heart is of the same proportions, so all is well. She calls us her children, and is moved to almost lyric expressions of pity for what she considers our sufferings, (her own are far greater). These utterances are balanced by very spirited broad comedy descriptions of the Hun. In the garden is a shell hole, two days old.

So we are having a useful rest. While we were having a "brunch" this morning, I saw Parish outside. He was bursting with news which he insisted we should discuss on the village green, as a precaution against spies behind the arras. We were given some very interesting and exciting information, after which he bounded off.

Cox and I went to a hill to have another look at the war and study our maps. We found things fairly active. Indeed it is extraordinary to think what a spectacle awaits anyone who cares to walk down the road.

I loved my few days at D.H.Q. The last night was at the time sensational, because the morrow was to have been a more remarkable day than it proved. We were in the office about eight o'clock when the General, as he went to his room, turned round, and, like a monarch tossing an honour to somebody, said in his regal manner, "Will Cox dine with us?" Parish, in his entirely Parishy way, beckoned to me and asked me to No. 2 mess. As we were titivating in his tent under the cedars he talked about what a good job we'd got, and said that if I hadn't done decently at the School I shouldn't have got it. They had to send to the School for the name of one officer to take on the business, and Molloy sent in my name, to my no small surprise, as I thought he wasn't best pleased with me. Dinner was as I say sensational, because I thought it would be the last meal in civilization for some time. The walls had some light paper, and there were heaps of candles. The meal was excellent, and there were charming people sitting about, and the gramophone played soft and sugary waltz tunes that were heavy with an atmosphere of ball-rooms and conservatories.

Parish is great fun. It was he who was attached to the Regiment that time as "gingerer-up extraordinary." Then he appeared mainly as the heavy soldier; now with close acquaintance he proves quite different. He is the naughty boy of the Staff, and in that office is a sort of bull in a china shop. He has tremendous energy and enthusiasm, but it emerges only in unconnected spurts. Also office work bores him. Now that I have seen him off his pedestal of the heavy soldier we get on very well.

I could tell you a dozen items of cheering news if it weren't for the censor.

JACK

I found this letter of Geoffrey's in my case. To-day is his birthday. How he would have enjoyed these times, and what notes we could have compared!

These are the last words he wrote to his family. The next day but one he went into action and did not return. He omitted to enclose the letter, but the case containing it was afterwards found on the battlefield, and came home on August 9th, the exact anniversary of Geoffrey's death at Hooge. The letter was written to his mother on April 13th, 1915, just as Geoffrey was starting from the Base Camp to join his Regiment, 2nd Sherwood Foresters, in the front line of the Ypres Salient, and in it he says, "Don't worry about me, all we have got to do is to wait a little." It seemed like a special message from the other side, coming on that day.

THE REST OF THE STORY, WHAT IS KNOWN OF IT, IS TOLD IN THE FOLLOWING LETTERS

From the Commandant Head Quarters School of Instruction

"YOUR son worked under me all last month, together with a number of other young Officers of the new armies whom I was training for the heavy responsibilities that must fall on their shoulders in this tremendous battle now being fought. He was quite the best, keenest, most hard-working and popular of them all, and I was very fond of him. As the time drew near we left our billets behind the line to take up our battle positions. In consequence of the favourable report I was able to give the Divisional Commander regarding your son he had been especially selected as one of the Forward Observing Officers, a post of considerable importance. I saw him the evening before he went into action, and I like to remember the cheery confidence he showed as we wished one another good luck.

As our troops rushed the German trenches opposite Ovillers your son followed on with an orderly. Half-way across No Man's Land he sent the orderly back with a message, and went on alone. Meanwhile our troops in that quarter had received very heavy punishment from machine guns, and finally were forced back. Your son, who was seen to enter the German trench, did not return with the survivors of the attack, and that is all we know. The adjacent ground was most carefully searched when it eventually fell into our hands, and all possible enquiries were made, but no trace of him was discovered. Both you and Mrs. Hoyle have my very deepest sympathy in your distress and anxiety. You have indeed given much for our Country and must be proud of your sons. Thank God England can still produce such lads, and may He bring consolation in time to Mrs. Hoyle and yourself in your sorrow."

From a General Staff Officer

" On July 1st, your son, one other officer, and some men were under my command, our duty being to act as Scouts and report the progress of the advance direct to the Division. I had made careful plans beforehand, and at a certain hour your son was to go forward into the German lines with a telephone, to a place hidden from us and report to me how things were going. At the time selected I thought the advance had not gone far enough to warrant his going forward, but I started him off an hour later with a telephone, two men to work it, and five other men, with orders to report himself personally to me again in three hours' time. My next information is all hear-say I am afraid, but I have made careful investigation and I believe I have the true story.

Your son went ahead with one man and told the others to follow with the telephone and the wire. The latter say they were unable to keep up, and lost sight of him behind a slight rise. They however pushed on into the front line with the wire, but did not see him again. The man who started with him went over our line, and half way across No Man's Land was sent back to me with a message. Your son went on by himself, and was not seen again. Presumably he meant to go on into the German trench and return to the telephone, which he thought would have by then reached our own front line.

At 3 p.m., about five hours after he left me, I heard that the men had not seen him since he had entered the German position, and that, though some of them had tried to get across, they had failed owing to the heavy fire the enemy were putting up.

Directly it was dark I took four men and went out beyond our front line, but I was unable to get into the German line, as they had by then re-occupied it, and I could find no trace of him. I wish I could do more to help him and you, and I offer you my deepest sympathy in the trial you are going through.

In the short time he was with me your son showed himself to be a very good officer, and he certainly acted as a most gallant gentleman in going forward alone into a place where he thought he ought not to take others and risk their lives, yet himself went on according to his orders."

Lightning Source UK Ltd.
Milton Keynes UK
171629UK00001B/62/P